Sweet Dreams
Sexuality Gender and Popular Fiction

Sweet Dreams

Sexuality Gender and Popular Fiction

edited by Susannah Radstone

LAWRENCE & WISHART
LONDON

Lawrence & Wishart Limited
39 Museum Street
London WC1A 1LQ

First published 1988

Photoset in North Wales by
Derek Doyle & Associates, Mold, Clwyd
Printed in Great Britain
at the University Printing House, Oxford

Contents

Acknowledgements

This book was originally envisaged as a follow up to 'The Left and the Erotic', edited by Eileen Phillips, and I would like to express my gratitude for her early work towards getting the project off the ground.

I would also like to thank the following people, without whom this collection would certainly have failed to see the light of day: the staff at Lawrence and Wishart, especially for their patience at those times when the path of editorship did not run smoothly; Richard Dyer for his concern and support; and Amal Treacher, whose affectionate encouragement made all the difference.

Introduction: Sweet Dreams and the Perverse Imagination

SUSANNAH RADSTONE

When we pause over the washing up or at parties and try to make sense of our lives and the way we've 'ended up', my friends and I sometimes agree and sometimes disagree over how best to explain the choices we've made and the way our lives have taken shape. Our partial, fragmentary and often contradictory explanations gesture towards our gender, our class and our ethnic and cultural backgrounds, but during these informal chats we often lay far greater stress on the influence of parents, lovers and friends. Some of us shrug and talk of the shaping force of chance encounters, while many of us also speak of the promptings of a diffuse desire for change. However, time and again, in accounting for the way our lives have taken shape, we return to the *novels* that we've read. Indeed, what continues to perplex and fascinate me is the force and urgency with which, in our search for influences, we repeatedly and emphatically refer to novels. In the common sense we make and share of the way our lives have taken shape, novels form landmarks, signals, reference points and sources of intense and lasting pleasure. They mean a lot to us. Sometimes we even say that they have 'changed our lives'.

But have particular novels really had such a huge impact upon us? And can it ever really be the case that novels have changed lives? This book is about the complex interplay between lives and novels. It focuses in particular on one specific area within that – that of the gendered reading of popular texts. More specifically, it raises questions about the relationship between changes in the ways we live as women and men, lesbian, gay and heterosexual, and those popular texts which are to a greater or lesser extent part of our lives. At the heart of all sexual politics lies a desire to celebrate and/or reconstitute our individual and collective identities. Where there are or have been social movements within which to live out these desires, particular novels, or genres of novel, have often been taken up as talismans and signposts around which we have gathered. Where there is no readily available wider community, or where access to a wider movement is restricted, novels frequently move centre stage, becoming crucial reference points. During the past few decades, a veritable explosion of women's, lesbian and gay novels have been snapped up and consumed by an apparently insatiable reading public. At the same time, sales of what might be described as the more longstanding popular genres have suffered no great decline. Instead, popular romantic fiction, for example, has sold increasingly massively of late.

Up until quite recently, the suggestion that both the traditional and the more marginal popular narratives should warrant serious critical attention would have raised quite a number of eyebrows. Indeed, it was generally assumed, (on the left, as well as within the more conservative enclaves of the academy), that popular narratives of the traditional type, such as romantic fiction, could be dismissed as 'mere ideology', or 'escapist pulp' ... the cheap glitter against which the silhouetted outlines of great literature could more easily be discerned, while gay, lesbian and women's fiction either remained entirely hidden, or was consigned to a dusty pile labelled 'of only marginal interest'. Moreover, Elizabeth Wilson suggests in her article on women's confessional narratives, that the new popular narratives, of, in this instance, the women's movement, share possibly problematic, as well as progressive elements with the more well established traditions of popular narrative and those of 'great literature'; this has the potential to unsettle not only the more conservative elements within literary criticism, but also those whose desire is to wholeheartedly celebrate those texts which have provided real support and inspiration in the attempt to live out the struggles and dreams of the lesbian, gay or women's movements. Nevertheless, changing forms of femininity and masculinity, in flesh and blood and in representation, occur as part of wider social changes, within which sexual politics is both the shaper and the shaped. While complex and difficult questions still remain concerning the exact nature of the relationship between that which is lived and that which is represented, the search for continuities and discontinuities between 'great literature', traditional popular narratives and lesbian, gay and women's novels can alert us to inconsistencies within an approach which seeks simply to replace that which appears 'regressive' with that which gets labelled 'progressive'. For example, in her essay on women's confessional writing, Elizabeth Wilson points out that these narratives share a rhetoric of intimate revelation with the work of such novelists as Philip Roth and John Salinger. That the novels of the women's movement can be shown to have been shaped, in part, by the same confessional rhetoric which marks the work of Salinger and Roth, suggests that the wholehearted celebration of the women's confessional novel might be tempered by an exploration of the wider social implications of the confession.

In a somewhat different vein, Alison Hennegan describes how, in her search for a sense of 'warmth, comfort, recognition and inclusion', she lit upon and cherished a selection of novels, which, at first sight, seem unlikely sources of inspiration for a young lesbian. Her 'cherished canon' included, for example, writers such as Jane Austen, Enid Blyton, Homer and Dickens – writers whose texts *she inflected* to fit the colours of her dreams.

Taken together, Hennegan's and Wilson's essays lend support to a profoundly circumspect approach to the compilation of an 'alternative canon' of lesbian, gay and women's novels, for while Wilson points to the potentially constraining force of one feature of much recent women's writing, Hennegan points up the unpredictability at the heart of the text/reader relations.

Indeed, in discussions amongst friends and with students, crucial similarities and differences in the sense we make of and the way we read novels have become apparent. Even where a group shares a similar recent history, the shadows of our less recent pasts also play their part in shaping the way in which a text gets read.

For instance, in conversations between myself and other women who entered higher education in their thirties, we have noticed that we share a common experience of having found Marilyn French's *The Women's Room* a significant text. Some of us say that it seemed to speak to us directly about a familiar world, or about an experience of femininity that was recognisably our own. Some say that the book provided support during a difficult transitional time. Yet though many of us *feel* that this novel has had a powerful influence on our lives, we are also unsure about how to gauge the status of that feeling. Perhaps we all refer to a novel because we want to feel like, or construct ourselves as 'bookish' women – after all, *The Women's Room* does suggest, amongst other things, that a proper passage to a new femininity is by way of books, by way of education. Or perhaps we refer to a novel as a way of addressing aspects of our experience that lie on the margins of our consciousness and that it would be difficult to address more directly. Or perhaps our sense of that novel as significant allows us to construct ourselves as 'free agents', after all, we chose to read that novel didn't we? Then again, perhaps the changes in our lives *together with The Women's Room* form part of a wider shift from one femininity to another, with our lives forming part of a transition which, given the benefit of a wider historical perspective, we might neither welcome nor seek to celebrate.

And then there is the question of the ways in which our less recent pasts play their part in shaping our reading patterns. In my own case, for instance, my responses to and feelings about particular novels are counterpointed by an awareness that novel reading *as a practice* had a specific meaning both within my family and later throughout my education. For me, novel reading was closely tied up, from an early age, with what it means to be a woman. Novel and poetry reading were my mother's way of saying 'I'm different' – a way of dissociating herself from her family background and later a route out from her cheerless and poverty-stricken marriage and away from the demands of two hungry daughters. Later, at secondary school, we girls were taught another way to read. In English classes we learned to search between the lines for traces of the author's soul. We learned to cherish these traces, for they bore testimony to our specially nurturing and 'sensitive' femininity.

For me then, the *very act* of novel reading will always partially evoke the shadows of this less recent past, and I offer this vignette as a corrective against the assumption that we can release the full meaning of a text from studying the words on the page. Indeed, I now find the mere sight of someone reading at a bus stop, on a plane, or in a train, both compelling and fascinating, since no inspection, no matter how intrusive, will reveal more than a book title, a few snatched sentences of text, or an absorbed expression – just scratches on the surface.

This collection forms part, however, of a recent move towards a rigorous intellectual exploration not just of the words on the pages of popular texts, but of the ways in which those texts mesh with our previously acquired cultural identities – an exploration whose aim then, is to shed light on those huddled reading figures. With the aid of theoretical insights culled from psycho-analysis, structuralism, semiotics and reader research, an attempt is now underway to move beyond an overly text-bound study of the relation between popular texts and the way in which we inhabit the world as women and men, towards an approach that can begin to take account of the ways we as readers *interact with*, shape and are shaped by particular texts.

At stake at the heart of this project lie a series of questions about the role of popular texts in the constitution or indeed re-constitution of femininity and masculinity – questions whose roots spread back to a wider 'popular culture' debate, in which competing readings of popular practices aim to produce the meaning/s of popular texts within the wider social world. Within this introduction it is not possible to offer a full account of the ways in which this debate informs these essays, but in the following remarks a little of the landscape surrounding each of the contributions collected here will be sketched in.

In the past, the study of popular texts has often focused on the potentially 'progressive' or 'regressive' aspects of a particular genre. Recently, however, such attempts at rigid categorisations have been unsettled, as more and more, theorists of popular culture have moved towards a position where the whole field of the 'popular' emerges as a terrain upon which struggles between dominant and oppositional meanings are constantly in progress. Similarly, the certainties of formalism, and an often Althusserian inspired structuralism, have been losing ground more recently in favour of a tendency which highlights the reader's role in shaping texts, and the ways in which class, gender, ethnicity – in short cultural context – all play their part in producing the sense we make of the texts we read. Moreover, it has also been repeatedly and insistently argued of late, that in order to gain even a limited insight into the ways in which popular texts appeal to us, then the pleasures of those texts must be interrogated to reveal the ways in which they intertwine with the real concerns, needs and desires of readers. Once pleasure had been placed at the top of the agenda, however, it soon became apparent that an analysis which revealed only the conscious desires awoken, spoken to or fulfilled by particular genres would be limited by its inability to address the ways in which those genres speak to our unconscious as well as our conscious reading selves. Psychoanalytically informed readings would, it was hoped, reveal new versions of the old stories about what it really means to be a man or a woman.

Of course, no single essay can hope to incorporate the full range of approaches that have recently been brought to bear on the study of sexuality, gender and popular texts. Each essay, therefore, has been chosen to illustrate one aspect of this field of research.

In commissioning these essays, I have also chosen to foreground work on lesbian and gay readings and texts. For many lesbians and gay men, especially those living in isolated situations, the discovery of a lesbian or gay novel, or even bookstore, can constitute a major turning point. In such circumstances, lesbian or gay novels really do seem to change lives. Yet reading lesbian or gay novels for the first time is often experienced as a 'homecoming' – a release from the tortuous and exhausting strategy of reading heterosexual novels 'against the grain'. But through which cracks do we learn to recognise ourselves in those first encounters with representations of lesbians and gay men, and how do we acquire the skill of 'reading against the grain'? For those of us who refuse to relegate lesbian and gay identities and practices to the level of 'the deviant' against which dominant culture etches out the parameters of acceptable heterosexual behaviour, seeking answers to such questions promises to bring to light the hidden instabilities at the heart of mainstream culture.

Nevertheless, though some of us do learn to read in our own ways, and to recognise ourselves in those first encounters with lesbian or gay novels, Jon Cook's essay 'Fictional fathers' warns us against underestimating the force with which mainstream culture works to address and position us within the parameters of acceptable heterosexuality. Cook's reading of popular romantic fiction weds Foucault to Freud to propose that the hero of popular romantic fiction represents paternal power, which, with the overturning of 'ancient' by 'modern' power, has retreated into a 'bizarre theatre of desire' played out within the family. Cook wishes to have done with fictional fathers; this mapping of complex patriarchal and social power relations onto the figure of the hero of popular romantic fiction describes the constraints which challenge the realisation of such wishes.

In 'What Is Life Without My Love?', Amal Treacher proposes that the hero of popular romantic fiction represents the 'maternal phallus', the ideal *mother and father* as fantasised by the infant. Treacher's reading of these novels produces one pointer towards a 'crack' at the heart of mainstream culture, for, *inter alia*, she suggests that popular romantic fiction speaks to its female readers' unconscious bisexual desires. While it might be argued that such 'whispers in the text' serve only to contain such perversity, their presence surely indicates a restlessness at the heart of mainstream culture.

At first glance it might appear that through their attempts to give voice to 'the truth' of women's experience, the feminist confessional novels of the 1970s and early 1980s amplified that restlessness within patriarchal relations. However, in 'Tell It Like It Is: Women and Confessional Writing', Elizabeth Wilson proposes that this very imperative sets limits upon the political potential of many women's autobiographical and fictional writing and its capacity to provide readers with real affirmation and support. Wilson argues that a return to the more distanced, ironic tone of Gertrude Stein's *Autobiography Of Alice B Toklas*, together with the inclusion, in our life stories, of ambiguity, uncertainty and a degree of incoherence, could subvert the confessional's pull towards fixing 'the truth' at the heart of the lives of 'heroines' or 'victims'. Unlike many postmodernist authors and literary critics, Wilson chooses to work with, rather than to dismiss the often urgently felt need amongst many readers, especially lesbians, for role models that can serve to support often unstable forms of femininity. In her questioning of the higher truth claimed for postmodernism's 'flux of identity and disintegration of experience', Wilson avoids merely reproducing the by now rather hackneyed call for 'the death of the author', suggesting that the take-up of such strategies, like the earlier enthusiasm for the realist confessional novel, could lead to the setting up of yet more modish imperatives.

Both Sally Munt's and Sara Lefanu's contributions to this collection share certain features in common with Elizabeth Wilson's essay. Like Wilson, Munt also seeks to make explicit the congruities between feminist writing and the wider culture of the mainstream. In her essay she argues that though lesbian crime novels are explicitly opposed to patriarchy, implicitly, 'they depend upon many aspects of the mainstream genre, such as an overriding Manichean morality of good versus evil, notions of unified subjectivity, innateness, natural justice, and tidy textual closures'. Munt's illustrative use of her own stories of reading lesbian crime fiction highlights a tension present in much lesbian and gay literary criticism informed by either a Foucauldian or a postmodern perspective – namely a tension between the *felt need* for affirmation, support and identification and an awareness of the difficulty of fulfilling these needs, without capitulating to the constraints of fixed subject positions and over-tidy narrative closures. This tension is anything but unproductive, however, for Munt argues that the best of these lesbian novels offer their readers a heroine figure who *plays* with identity, and a sense of community within which interdependence and a blurring of boundaries prefigure, perhaps, the world of our dreams.

In 'Robots and Romance' Sara Lefanu echoes Wilson in arguing that Tanith Lee's use of irony and wit combine to undercut whatever might otherwise tend towards conservatism in the ways in which science fiction's subgenres of fantasy and sword and sorcery represent gender and sexuality. Here again then, it turns out that certainly where questions of sexual politics are concerned, hard and fast distinctions between 'conservative' and 'radical' genres do not hold. Instead, Lefanu leaves us with the proposal that perhaps it is the formulaic nature of these subgenres that leaves the way open for their ironic interrogation.

Similarly, in 'Children of the Night', Richard Dyer argues that at different historical moments, the vampire novel has served to denigrate and to celebrate homosexuality. He suggests that 'there is a fit between the values and feelings explored and produced by the vampire genre and the values and feelings of emergent lesbian and gay identities in the 19th and 20th centuries', and goes on to propose that 'while in all vampire fiction, vampirism can be taken to evoke the thrill of forbidden sexuality, whereas earlier examples express horror and revulsion at it, later examples turn this on its head and celebrate it'. This continuing appeal of the vampire image must, he concludes, indicate that vampirism represents 'something about homosexual desire that remains stubbornly marginal, unruly, fascinating and indispensable'. This carefully detailed study of changing inflections within the vampire genre leads Dyer to propose a reciprocal relationship between *lived* sexual identities (here specifically homosexual), and the wider culture – between 'how others have thought about us and how we have thought about ourselves'. This proposal allows space for a guarded optimism, for, in the right circumstances, it's clear that the shaping power of the perverse imagination will continue to transform shadows into sweet dreams.

But how much do we yet know about the mechanisms of that perverse imagination, and the particular circumstances which facilitate its operation. And does it operate in opposition or as counterpoint to that mainstream culture which still massively shapes our identities as women and as men?

In the final essay in this collection, 'On Becoming a Lesbian Reader', Alison Hennegan returns to her early memories of reading to reconstruct the origins and formation of her own 'perverse imagination'. Hennegan describes how she came to collect for herself a personal popular canon of novels which she used as sources of comfort and support as she strove, as an adolescent, to come to terms with her lesbianism. In a wonderfully evocative passage, she tells of how she became adept at finding *her* books – 'I became aware of and learned to rely on a phenomenon which I can only call a pricking of my thumbs, a capacity which led me, unfailingly and time and time again, to the 'right' book for me, however unlikely its disguise'. One page on, Hennegan adds that this sensation condensed 'a complex system of noticing and connecting a myriad of facts usually deemed irrelevant or insignificant ...' A perfect description of the 'perverse imagination' at work.

One of the most enduring and endlessly perplexing questions for cultural theory is how, in a world suffused by dominant messages, apparently oppositional signals manage to sneak into the public arena. One response is to argue that on the whole, what appears oppositional, has, in fact, been deployed by dominant culture to act as decoy. Within this framework, whatever exists as representation has always already been recuperated for dominant culture. In the field of gender/sexuality and popular culture, I believe that taken together, the essays collected here suggest that such a gloomy picture is both inaccurate as well as inappropriate. What this volume points to, rather, are some of the ways in which, as readers and writers, we can, to some extent, begin to shape the world that we want out of the bricks and mortar that surround us. Many questions remain concerning the relation between these dreams, the perverse imagination that produces them, and the wider culture to which they are inextricably related. Yet Hennegan's story illustrates the way in which we as readers, as well as as writers, can and do perform complex acts in our effort to produce other stories. Moreover, the desire to find other ways to inhabit the world does not, in itself, spring from nothingness, for, as this collection insists, the popular novels of the mainstream can also be shown to tell more than one story.

Tell It Like It Is: Women and Confessional Writing

ELIZABETH WILSON

My interest in autobiographical writing developed out of an autobiographical work of my own: *Mirror Writing*.[1] This began as an intellectual exploration of the concept of identity, which I illustrated with fragments of autobiography. These were then expanded and given a more linear narrative form – but this very process moved the book towards a form which arouses certain expectations and of which it was actually an implicit critique: the feminist confessional – an account of struggle, a moral tale, the exemplary charting of a woman's 'born again' progress.

I wanted to interrogate feminists' attitudes towards both feminine and feminist identities. One impulse that led me to *Mirror Writing* arose from the unease I felt (and still feel) with the identity of 'feminist'. For not only the world at large but also other feminists seemed to interpret this as a kind of character armour unfractured by doubt or vulnerability. No chink in her armour for a feminist; she must be a heroine, a warrior-woman, an inspiration to others. I felt oppressed and damaged by the stereotype. I felt strongly that the protagonist(s) or author of a feminist work should not have to embody feminist virtues in the way that western art for centuries has used the female form to represent uplifting abstract qualities.[2] I wanted something different; I wanted to write about experience freed from the imperative of affirmation, to explore ambiguity, complexity and the 'politically incorrect', to escape the twin poles of suffering and triumph which

21

constitute the approved feminist trajectory. For it is the journey from victim to heroine that characterises feminist confessional writing, and I was neither.

I also wanted, both in *Mirror Writing* and in a more recent piece of fictional, but still personal writing, *Prisons of Glass*[3] to explore what I experience as a gap or a mismatch in feminist writing. This is the gap between life as we live it and life as we believe it ought to be lived; between inchoate desire and the clarity of understanding; between moments of sheer joy and knowledge of suffering and horror – it is about the impossibility of reconciling all the contradictions in our lives.

Contemporary feminism is rich in two kinds of writing especially: the theoretical and the experiential. These are, indeed, two sides of the same coin, the one investigating the other: 'raw experience' is marshalled into intellectual coherence and given a pattern within feminist theory, while confessional writing rebels against the élitism and distance of academic discourse and returns women's experience to its immediacy. But, whatever else, 'feminist' writing must ultimately be political; and yet this agitational imperative may cause tensions both in academic and in experiential writing, since polemic may go against the grain of the objectivity and neutrality of academic norms, while it may also reduce the complexity of our lived experience to a flat and one-dimensional caricature. In both kinds of writing, different levels of experience may not easily be brought together. The level of political beliefs and commitment, rational and purposeful, is not so easily brought into line with the mass of feelings, intuitions, fantasies, obsessions, nor with the 'trivial', lost and evanescent moments of daily life, the bits and pieces of half-forgotten memories (the fragments that Freud called 'the refuse of the phenomenal world'). Can these moments – perhaps what make life most precious – be brought within 'the political'? Should they be?

I'm not sure how deliberately the feminists of the late 1960s and early 1970s chose the genres in which we would speak our oppression. In the beginning I suspect we just plunged in, seeking what was nearest to hand as a vehicle for our explanations.

A literature of explanation and of testimony. I shall not explore the history of theory here, but the history of the autobiographical mode is interesting in view of its use by feminists. It is impossible, actually, to arrive at any strict definition of autobiography, or clearly to mark it off from autobiographical fiction, or to make absolute distinctions between fiction and truth; the scholarship that has been devoted to just this demarcation of genres seems to miss the point. For not only is much fiction autobiographical; all autobiography is in some sense fictional – the remembrance or the searching again for the 'lost times' is never just an act of memory or research, but is inevitably a re-creation, something new.

On the other hand the labels determine audience expectation, readers expecting a kind of 'truth' or revelation from autobiography not expected from fiction in quite the same way. Or perhaps they expect 'revelation' from autobiography and 'truth' from fiction, so that autobiography can become devalued by being associated with gossip and scandal.

The tradition from which both autobiography and the nineteenth century novel developed was nevertheless one and the same. Historians locate the origins of both kinds of writing in the dual cultural movements of the 16th and 17th centuries: the Renaissance and the Reformation:

> In the seventeenth century there is clear ... evidence for a new interest in the self, and for recognition of the uniqueness of the individual. This is a development common to Europe, and which apparently has its origins in two different strands of thought: the secular Renaissance ideal of the individual as hero as expressed in the autobiography of Cellini or the essays of Montaigne; and religious introspection arises from the Calvinist sense of guilt and anxiety about salvation ...
>
> There developed a series of almost wholly new genres of writing, the intimately self-revelatory diary, the autobiography and the love letter. Partly, of course, these products were the result of a shift from an oral to a written culture among the laity. Literacy is probably a necessary pre-condition for the growth of introspection.[4]

Alternatively:

according to Lacan, the development of the modern '*Je*' was encouraged by the manufacture of mirrors. Blown glass mirrors were first manufactured on a commercial scale in Venice in the sixteenth century and plate-glass mirrors became available and cheap early in the eighteenth century. So whereas medieval man [sic] can only have had fleeting and blurred impressions of his own body, modern man can see himself clearly in mirrors and has opportunities for entrancing encounters with his own image. It is therefore tempting to correlate the enormous increase in the production of autobiographies in this century with the technological changes that have enabled people to make physical self-scrutiny a daily bathroom event and to see – and hear – themselves as others see them.

But maybe ... it was really all the other way round ... [maybe it was the] ... greater self-awareness that created the demand for mirrors and the impetus to invent cameras, films and tape-recorders.[5]

In either case the confessional mode is ambiguous, since the writer who engages in it is both embarking upon a self-critical act of introspection – searching for identity, questing for authenticity – and simultaneously putting her/himself forward as exemplary, admirable, different.

It has been left to women critics to point out that the 17th century writings cited by Lawrence Stone were particularly likely to be written by women. Some feminists have even claimed that these fragmentary, private and personal modes of writing are peculiarly women's genres because they reflect the interrupted, fragmentary and private nature of women's experience.[6]

But it is also the case that out of these genres developed the 19th century realist novel, a genre to some extent launched by Samuel Richardson, a man. In *Pamela*[7], published in 1740, he used the epistolary or letter form to tell a story about an attempted seduction in which master pursues maidservant. The details of the pursuit are prurient, but love and good fortune triumph when the would-be seducer finally marries Pamela. Yet despite this Mills and Boon ending, the novel is realistic, although it simultaneously offers a role model of virtuous womanhood: Richardson was writing for an expanding female audience, and his intention was didactic. *Pamela* was therefore, like much feminist writing today, exemplary, although the virtues set forth were those proposed for women by the dominant bourgeois culture, whereas feminist writings purport to be counter-cultural works.

John Cleland's *Fanny Hill*,[8] written, also in letter form, a few years after *Pamela* and in deliberate parody of it, likewise describes a young woman's experience. Fanny Hill, however, unlike Pamela, succumbs to her seducer; she is a whore and *Fanny Hill* is an erotic novel, in which the author draws on the anti-clericalism and materialism of contemporary French literature to imply 'a view of nature and natural feelings, including the erotic, as a substitute for religion and metaphysics'.[9] Sexuality, for Cleland, represented a kind of privileged truth, and in its graphic description of sexuality his novel in some ways anticipated what was to re-emerge in the late nineteenth century as 'Naturalism'.

Rousseau inaugurated a new level of shameless *self*-revelation in his autobiography. *The Confessions*[10] published in 1780, aimed to portray the author in what Cleland had called 'stark, naked truth' – Rousseau's was *not* an exemplary enterprise, except in so far as he was aiming to be truthful. The anti-hero was thus born in this confessional mode.

But both novels and autobiographies have developed around the idea of a central character, a hero or heroine, often an idealised character, but most importantly one with whom the reader can identify. Novel and autobiography have grown from a common root. Both were also traditionally realistic. In the 20th century, however, many novelists have abandoned realism. The 'naturalism' which followed 19th century realism could in any case encompass some of the fragmentation of experience that modernism was to develop. Writers of the naturalist school dwelt on the minutiae of daily life until both reader and characters could seem lost and fragmented in the whirlpool of endless, meaningless sensation offered by life in the modern metropolis. This then led to the modernist exploration of the fragmentation and questioning of identity and self.[11]

Psychoanalysis, too, introduced a whole new dimension to the concept of 'confession', and explored the way in which the recollection of the past involves a constant reworking of the notion of 'self'. If the real-life self is a fiction formed out of memory (which changes through time), repressed desire and the demands of the external world, then the fictional identity of the narrator *and* the protagonist of the autobiographical presentation become equally suspect.

The recovery of the past and the understanding of the self reveal 'truth' as a far more ambiguous concept than the realist narrative, whether fictional or autobiographical, would have had us believe. And the 20th century blurring of genres has been not so much a return to the realism which created an illusion of fiction as 'truth', as the exploration of 'reality' as 'really' fictional.

Critical approaches to autobiography have changed to match its changing development.[12] There has been a shift from autobiography seen as a source of truth – an emphasis on its exemplary and didactic function – towards an aknowledgement of autobiography as literature. In its modernist form this becomes the deconstruction of the 'I' of identity of the writing self, a critique of essentialist concepts of self, and modernist autobiography exemplifies in literary form the belief that identity is socially constructed and therefore changing over time, rather than consisting of an essence unchanging throughout a lifetime.

Although in recent years feminists have returned to the novel – to such an extent that there now exists a distinct sub-genre, the 'feminist novel' – it was not with the novel but with the theoretical work that the 'second wave' of feminism began – with Simone de Beauvoir's *The Second Sex*[13] and Betty Friedan's *The Feminine Mystique*.[14] Yet in the period immediately prior to the 'rebirth' of feminism there was a flourishing international literary tradition of the interrogation of personal experience through fiction, often autobiographical fiction.

In the 1960s the outspokenness of the deviant was prized in literature. Williams Burroughs and Alexander Trocchi wrote about their lives as drug addicts, John Reechy and Hubert Selby wrote about homosexuality, violence and rape. Fiction shaded into pornography in the confrontation of 'ugly' truths. Truth, deviance and sexuality coalesced into a counter-cultural, dissident discourse.

In the same period English women novelists such as Margaret Drabble and Edna O'Brien were reworking the traditional novel, in the tradition of an earlier generation – Elizabeth Taylor, Rosamund Lehmann and many others.[15] Theirs was a tradition of realism in which middle and upper middle class domestic life was explored in all its emotional minutiae, and there is a stoicism about many of these novels, the authors depicting with stark, hyper-realist clarity, the details of narrow lives and intensely experienced although often stifled emotions.

But there was also Doris Lessing's *The Golden Notebook*[16] which was to become a key text, particularly for the American women's movement. And this, along with the translation of Simone de Beauvoir's autobiographies, appeared to express a widespread desire among women for an autonomous identity *as women*. These autobiographical heroines embodied the quest for the answer to the question echoing down the century: what does it mean to be a woman? What does Woman want?

So both the breaking of taboos in writing, mostly by men, about drugs, deviant sexuality and violence, and the strong women's voice in the literature of the 1960s, opened up possibilities and created the preconditions for an explosion of explicitly feminist writing in the 1970s. The women's movement erupted, beginning as a politics of experience, and what seemed important then, at the beginning, was for women to 'find a voice' and to testify to an experience that had been lost, silenced or never even allowed to emerge into consciousness.

Directly experiential and personal writing was seen as political rather than literary; indeed, there may have been a rejection of the whole conventional artistic enterprise as

women seized on the confessional genre as a way of giving
consciousness-raising a more permanent form. In this
writing, women expressed their 'radical otherness' and
'made strange' the familiar world by reason of their angle
of vision. Theirs were to be narratives of truth, and
women were to bear witness to the authenticity of their
lives, a hidden and neglected truth, but all the more
subversive for that reason – the testimony now finding
expression would cast a new light on the accepted truths of
the male world.

There was, in fact, a European precedent for the avant
garde and explicitly political use of personal testimony and
the confessional in the German radical movements of the
1960s. They insisted on both the retelling of personal
experience and the sharing of it in political groups: and
this bringing of personal experience to the centre of the
political stage was enthusiastically taken up by the German
women's movement.

Two of the most successful pieces of confessional
writing were Anja Meulenbelt's *The Shame is Over*[17] from
Holland, and Verena Stefan's *Shedding*,[18] both best sellers.
(*Shedding* is described on the cover of the American edition
as 'the bible of the German women's movement'.) Each of
these books charts the progress of a young woman against
the background of the 'sexual revolution' of the early 60s
and the women's and students' movements of the late
1960s and early 1970s: a journey from a false self to a new
'feminist' self. To read *Shedding* in 1985, however (ten
years after its original publication) is to read a text that
seems dated, the ideologies of the early women's
movement revealed as crude and unsatisfactory. The
heroine-narrator moves through a series of relationships
which correspond to her development as a feminist, from
sexual subjection to autonomy. She has a relationship with
a black man, and one with a leftist radical, and in both
cases sexual relations with men are shown as heavy,
oppressive and humourless. Worse, neither the black man,
despite his own oppression, nor the radical, despite his
politics, can even begin to understand the heroine's desire
for liberation. The heroine moves forward to a lesbian

relationship, but this also fails. The two women seem to feel no spontaneous mutual sexual attraction, and eventually take refuge in the idea that their relationship is a maternal one; however the ideology of motherhood is not explored, nor does there seem any awareness that the equation of lesbian with maternal feeling is a cliché of conservative psychoanalytic thought. There is a gap between the relationship described and the rhetoric of the period about 'women loving women' so that the effect of this part of the book is of dishonesty or equivocation, just as there now seems in the section devoted to the male lovers a sullen refusal to grant them any authenticity – women's oppression is the only reality, and left politics and the oppression of black men are judged as not merely insignificant by comparison with women's oppression, but the seriousness with which they take themselves is seen as intrinsically male. Ultimately the feminist protagonist's acceptance of herself as an autonomous woman involves a view of *all* relationships as constraining and restrictive; by the end of the book she is alone, and celibate solitude is implicitly advanced as the goal of the search for selfhood, an ending similar to that of Rosamund Lehmann's 1927 bestseller, *Dusty Answer*:

> She was going home again to be alone. She smiled, thinking suddenly that she might be considered an object for pity, so complete was her loneliness.
> One by one they had all gone from her ... She was rid at last of the weakness, the futile obsession of dependence on other people. She had nobody now except herself; and that was best.[19]

This is a recognisable moment in the life of many young middle class women. They may savour that moment of coming to adulthood and freedom from intimate relationships even more sharply than young men, since family intimacy *is* often restrictive for women, and since the moment of freedom is brief. For most, renewed confinement in a new family is what the future will offer.

As a political solution, however, solitude is hardly sufficient.

In Anja Meulenbelt's *The Shame is Over* the heroine's development is also charted through sexual relationships, from traditional marriage, traversing 'sexual liberation' to lesbianism. Yet Rosalind Coward, writing about 'feminist novels' and 'feminist autobiographies' points out that 'the centrality attributed to sexual consciousness has always been a potential problem in feminist novels for it seems to reproduce the dominant ways in which women are defined in this society – through their sexual relationships'.[20] Since, however, contemporary feminism has seen sexuality as at the core of women's oppression, it is difficult to avoid placing it at the centre of the feminist confessional, for feminism has carried over from the wider culture the belief that our sexual being is the core of ourselves, where our identity most fundamentally resides.

Rosalind Coward argues that as the feminist novel/ feminist autobiography has become more predictable it has lost all political edge, and that 'transparent' writing (realism) 'where the heroine just moves unanalytically through experiences, is much more likely to end up endorsing dominant ideologies than questioning them'. For her, Alison Fell's autobiographical novel *Every Move You Make*[21] is little more, at times, than a counter cultural Mills and Boon in which men 'find the heroine compellingly attractive' while she herself gains neither affirmation nor insight from these relationships, but simply heads for breakdown for reasons neither she nor the reader can understand. This can then be read, Rosalind Coward argues, as a moral tale against the dangers of the 1970s counter-culture with its half-baked notions of multiple relationships, sexual experimentation and drug abuse.

Alison Fell's book could, however, be seen as an attempt to get beyond the other dimension of confessional writing: the imperative of affirmation. For confessional writing testifies to an ideological pressure to 'celebrate' women and womanhood. The danger then is that some kind of female essence is reconstructed, and the idea that there exists a wholly Other set of 'women's values' and that women are entirely different from and morally superior to men is reproduced. Since this is one aspect of the dominant ideology about women, the cutting edge of the feminist *critique* of femininity and 'womanliness' is lost.

The confessional writings of black women and lesbians are especially relevant when we consider Affirmation. Because both groups suffer from a double (or triple if working class) oppression, it has been especially important for black and lesbian writers to reject the stereotypes of the dominant culture. A feminist writer who is black or a lesbian *must* say that it is not bad, sick, inferior or contemptible to *be* black or lesbian. Yet at the same time the charting of her life experience will almost inevitably involve an account of the internalisation of stereotypes and the self hatred of the oppressed in our society. To speak frankly of difficulty and pain is, however, to court criticism. Catharine Stimpson's *Class Notes*[22] for example, is about the discovery by the heroine in the 1950s that she is a lesbian, a topic involving the recognition of self hatred and guilt. But she and other lesbian authors have been roundly criticised for reproducing these mechanisms of self oppression rather than celebrating their condition:

> Several dominant themes recur in these books; the common factor is that all in some way disempower the lesbian ... In these novels we do not read about what we have found in our lesbian relationships – the intimacy, the support.[23]

This dilemma in relation to the writings of black women has been explored by Selwyn Cudjoe in his discussion of Maya Angelou's autobiographical writing.[24] He tells us that the tradition from which Maya Angelou speaks is a specifically Afro-American form: 'During the eighteenth century and nineteenth century thousands of autobiographies of Afro-American slaves appeared expressing their sentiments about slavery'[25]. Cudjoe emphasises the moral purpose of this type of autobiography; it is a *political* project, the purpose of which is to bear witness to the sufferings of a people, as 'one of the most important means of negotiating our way out of the condition of enslavement and as a means of expressing the intensity with which Afro-American people experience their *violation* and *denigration*.' He goes on to say:

> The Afro-American autobiographical statement as a form tends to be bereft of any *excessive subjectivism* and *mindless* egotism. Instead it presents the Afro-American as reflecting a much more *im-personal* condition, the autobiographical subject emerging as an almost random member of the group ... as a consequence [it] emerges as a *public* rather than a *private* gesture ... and superficial concerns about *individual subject* usually give way to the *collective subjection* of the group.[26]

Cudjoe, that is, emphasises the exemplary aspect of autobiography, and denigrates the exploration of subjectivity. Yet because he comes down so strongly on the side of an ethical and political statement that must always celebrate the dignity of an oppressed group and never allow us to forget society's oppression, he finds it difficult to integrate *Gather Together in My Name*,[27] in which the author describes her life as a young woman in an underworld of pimps, prostitutes and petty crooks: 'Its lack of moral weight and ethical centre deny it an organising principle and rigour capable of keeping the work together'.[28] But the writer's later development and ultimate success testify, Cudjoe asserts, to 'her evolution as an autonomous and fully liberated person' and he feels that she achieves 'an organic harmony of her personal history as it intertwined with the social history of her people' and that it also bears witness 'to the personal triumph of a remarkable black woman. *Singin' and Swingin'* is a celebration of that triumph'.[29]

Feminists seem to have accepted uncritically this emphasis – which is American rather than specifically black – on the desirability of role models and heroines, and the general assumption that the celebration of individual success and the individual's triumph over adversity must represent a political position that is unproblematically progressive from a feminist perspective. But while I accept that it may be inspiring to read about women whose personal success has been the paradigm of a triumph of determination and character over personal misfortune and the injustices of a sexist and racist class society, this very enterprise carries with it the individualism of the unjust society itself. On the one hand, as another critic expresses it, Maya Angelou's autobiography is 'not a singular statement of individual egotism but an exultant explorative revelation that she *is* because her life is an inextricable part of the misunderstood reality of who Black people and Black women truly are'. Yet on the other hand, 'that "self" is the model which she holds before Black women'.[30]

As Margaret Walters perceptively demonstrated in her discussion of Simone de Beauvoir, the 'exemplary' life must inevitably embody values and assumptions that other women in different places and times may not endorse.[31] Mary Evans, too, points out that Simone de Beauvoir's life is, without too much difficulty, assimilable into a highly individualistic idea of what women's emancipation is about.[32] At the worst, as Helen Taylor has suggested, the promotion of women writers as role models becomes confused with mere publicity and may turn into 'the most suspect kind of heroine worship' and 'the problem for radical readers and critics is that the obsession with the author rather than the text has been rightly identified as a bourgeois preoccupation which has worked against women's interests'.[33]

Insofar as the feminist autobiographer puts herself forward as the exceptional woman who paradoxically typifies the problems faced by a whole generation of women, she creates herself as a *star*. The role of the star is to represent in a condensed form certain of the irresolvable social conflicts in a society and to provide a 'solution' to them in ideology. S/he and audience together create a magical solution to insoluble difficulties, and 'these star-audience relationships are only an intensification of the conflicts and exclusions experienced by everyone'.[34] That is to say the conflicts may be *simultaneously* highlighted and smoothed over by the 'star' representation and this may also be the effect of some confessional writings: both to express and magically to solve dilemmas. This makes their challenge to the status quo at best partial.

There is also the danger that the feminist heroine will be lifted out of her specific time and place and given a false universalism. In discussing Simone de Beauvoir Mary Evans points to some of the dangers of this:

> It would seem that in its search for universal explanations, and definitions, of women's subordination, feminism is ... deeply attracted by the idea of a universal, trans-historical feminist: a feminist for all cultures and all political systems ...
>
> To mythologize de Beauvoir is ... to diminish her. As a life-long champion of the Left, and of civil rights and liberties for women and minorities, she is one of the most eminent and courageous figures of the twentieth century; as a champion of 'freedom' or 'choice' for women, she becomes a manipulable symbol for many of those beliefs and ideologies within the West that diminish human freedom.[35]

Perhaps lesbians need an affirmative identity even more than black women, for the lesbian sense of self is particularly vulnerable. Black women and men can identify strongly with anti-imperialist struggles all over the world, they can look historically to black cultures, and, like women, they are, in global terms, not a minority. Lesbians *are* a minority and have necessarily lived a culturally marginal existence. Unlike blacks or women, lesbians may hide their identity, nor is it always a permanent one. It may therefore be a more vulnerable identity than those others. (To state this is not to seek to place them at the top of some hierarchy of oppressions, but rather to re-emphasise the diversity of female experience and oppression, a diversity with different *political* conse-quences for different groups.) Precisely because of its instability and – sometimes – secrecy, affirmation is particularly important for the lesbian identity, yet lesbians too need the space not only to voice their oppression and their determination to transcend it, but also to explore uncertainty, ambiguity and vulnerability.

In any case, since most women cannot possibly achieve the fame and success of a Maya Angelou, a Rita Mae Brown or a Simone de Beauvoir, the whole enterprise may go astray. The force of their examples may inhibit or depress rather than inspire.

'Heroinization' also fixes the role model heroine in what may be invidious ways. In Holland in 1985, two Dutch lesbian friends said to me – on separate occasions but with the same wry smile, and using almost the same words – 'Oh – Anja Meulenbelt's relating to men again – she's "come out" as a heterosexual!' Does the new truth annul the inspirational confession of the past? What happens if a role model changes course and herself no longer identifies with the certainties of a past decade?

The role model is a highly selective representation, and elevation to a pedestal is often followed by being knocked off it again when further, incompatible truths emerge. Angela Davis points out that Gertrude Stein was guilty of racist stereotyping in one of her novels,[36] and the homophobic stereotypes of lesbians in Maya Angelou's *Gather Together in My Name* are even more shocking, given that they are so much more recent. Once, lesbians identified with the tragic, romantic heroine of Radclyffe Hall's *Well of Loneliness*[37], but today we are shocked to discover that Radclyffe Hall herself was warmly sympathetic to the Italian Fascist Party. In the end, all heroines have feet of clay.

Inevitably. For to elevate women to the status of heroine is to do both them and ourselves a horrible and mutilating injustice. To demand of other women that they be wonderful on our behalf is to see them as abstractions, not as women, and is to deny them something that Anja Meulenbelt herself identified as important: the right to try new identities, new ways of living and new forms of relationship – and to *fail*. And all writing, including political writing, must question the meaning of experience and cannot rest content with a preconceived 'right answer'. The certainties of affirmation are always only half truths.

It must be that many women read Anja Meulenbelt and
Verena Stefan with an instant recognition of their own
oppression and pain, yet that very identification with the
problem might make reasoned criticism of the unsatisfactory analysis of the problems (in Verena Stefan's book
especially) difficult or impossible. Yet the conclusion
reached by both books – the emphasis on 'loving women'
as a means of enhancing *self-esteem*, an idea culled
ultimately from popular psychotheraphy (the idea that by
learning to love yourself you will be better able to relate to
the world, and that you learn to love yourself by having a
good 'role model'), although not entirely misconceived, is a
voluntaristic and apolitical response. Moreover, neither
book gives sufficient emphasis to the reality of many
women's lives (even white, middle class ones) in which the
main problems are not just, or perhaps not mainly, men
and relationships, but social and economic constraints.
Although these were counter-cultural works, they tended
to substitute for dominant ideologies about women
feminist truisms which acted in terms of closure, rather
than opening out and encouraging a deepened understanding and questioning of experience.

Their form remained in some ways rather conventional,
and unquestioned. The imperative to 'tell it like it is' never
allowed for ambiguity, still less for an ironic approach that
seemed out of keeping with contemporary feminist
politics. For irony is essentially anti-heroic, and, 'in the
ironic discourse, every position undercuts itself, thus
leaving the politically engaged writer in a position where
her ironic discourse might just come to deconstruct her
own politics'.[38] It has also by now become quite a cliché to
point out that this deconstruction of identity may, if
applied to womanhood, call into question the whole
project of a feminist movement itself; what unity can be
organised around a fragmented identity?

Yet although Radclyffe Hall's lesbian heroine was
doomed and tragic, it may be that the lesbian or
homosexual identity has more often been an ironic
comment on the norms of heterosexuality, exposing the
heavy-handedness of masculine and feminine stereotypes,

often with great wit, both in life and in literature. The confessional form has tended to be conservative stylistically, usually relying on a realist narrative, while the range of emotions – anguish, anger, triumph – excludes comedy or mockery. The work of Gertrude Stein, however – popular with some feminists in the United States, but largely ignored by them in Britain, I think – brings together modernism and gay irony. *The Autobiography of Alice B Toklas*[39] also questions the nature of autobiographical writing itself:

> Even the title page of the current Vintage edition – *The Autobiography of Alice B Toklas* by Gertrude Stein – is enough to suggest that the centre of the ensuing text may be difficult to locate. The original Harcourt edition made the same point in a more subtle way: both the cover and the title page print only a title – *The autobiography of Alice B Toklas* – but no author's name is given. The frontispiece (facing the title page) however, is a Man Ray photograph which shows Stein in the right foreground, seated at a table, but with her back to the camera and in dark shadow; Alice B Toklas stands in the left background, but she stands in light and framed by a doorway. The photograph, with its obscure foreground and distinct background, has no clear primary subject – like the book that follows; the seated Stein, however, is writing, and the possibility is raised that *she* may be the author of the book, an uncertainty not resolved for the reader of this edition until its final page – when 'Toklas' tells us that Stein has in fact written *The Autobiography*.[40]

The book inverts the conventions of autobiography in focussing largely on the friends of Alice B Toklas and Gertrude Stein – the famous painters with whom they associated – and has nothing to say about emotions, relationships or aspirations, normally the meat of autobiography. The whole idea of 'character' is jettisoned and the flavour of their life together is recreated by description of the outward, anecdotal and inconsequential details of daily life. At the same time the book does obliquely explore the ambiguities of a lesbian relationship and the masculine and feminine role playing within it at a time when this could hardly be dismissed openly. Indeed the book implicitly questions our contemporary assumption that direct revelation, 'the stark, naked truth' *is* necessarily 'the truth'.

Yet if the confessional form has led some feminist writers away from such questioning, this is certainly not true of feminist theoretical writing. Some feminist theorists have immersed themselves in the Freudian tradition precisely because it is a theory of how subjectivity is constructed and because it suggests that this construction is always tentative, fragmented, a kind of necessary fiction. Some have engaged in empirical work, participating in in-depth interviewing of other women to capture a wider, perhaps more representative experience. Others have done 'action research' or used symbolic interaction or phenomenological approaches. All these have seemed to open fruitful possibilities for non-élitist investigations in which to ground a feminist theory that would be true to democratic feminist ideals.

There has also been a consistent attempt by feminists to crash the genre barriers altogether. Some of the early women's liberationists interrogated and moved away from their original academic or academic-political orientation. In *Women's Consciousness Man's World*,[41] for example, Sheila Rowbotham combined theoretical with personal writing to describe what it felt like to be a young woman growing up 'under capitalism' and at the same time to relate this to the marxist feminist analysis of how women were positioned within the social formation. She does not discuss the need for a new genre that would fuse theoretical and confessional writing, but she does argue that the enterprise requires a whole new *language*, for:

> Our oppression is more internalised – the clumsiness of women penetrates the very psyche of our being. It is not just a question of being outside existing language. We can never hope to enter and change it from inside. We can't just occupy existing words. We have to change the meanings of words before we take them over ... The exclusion of women from all existing language demonstrates our profound alienation from any culture which can generalise itself.[42]

Kate Millett, whose *Sexual Politics*[43] had started out as a PhD thesis but became a best seller, rejected academic discourse entirely thereafter. Her next book was a brief collection of testimonies by prostitutes. In her introduction to *The Prostitution Papers* she contrasted an academic way of writing with the new straight-from-the-heart style she had now adopted:

> I no longer clung to that bleak pretence of objectivity routinely required of PhD candidates ... My language had to reflect the experience itself: colloquial, excited, immediate ... I was writing at last out of direct emotional involvement. I began to write the way I talk and feel.[44]

She concludes this paragraph with the words 'In short I learnt how to write', which casts a more ambiguous light on her preceding remarks, since it acknowledges the amount of *art* required in the development of a seemingly immediate style, a style, moreover, that in this case she is using to reproduce the 'voice' of other women – the prostitutes she interviewed – and she acknowledges that 'for all the voices it took a good deal of work to transform spoken to linear language'. She has since written two autobiographical novels.[45] These acknowledge a debt to *The Golden Notebook* in their attempt to include *everything* in a stream of consciousness that, far from celebrating the protagonist's triumph over circumstances, involves the reader in her pain, her failures and her depression in the midst of great outward 'success'. Like *The Golden Notebook* these works are about the distress and difficulty of being an independent self-activated woman in our society.

Recently, several books have been published that have been made up of personal accounts by different women, but around a theme that is shared. One such is *Breaking Silence*[46], accounts by nuns and ex-nuns of their discovery of lesbianism within the cloister. Many brief fragments coalesce into a testimony that gives a strong sense of the contradictory pull of sexuality and religion – and of some of the connexions between the two. *Truth Dare or Promise: Girls Growing up in the Fifties*[47] brings together the recollections of women brought up in the optimistic aura of 'the postwar vision of prosperity and limitless possibilities' who then came to feminism in the more hostile political climate of the 1970s and 1980s. The testimonies are all different; as the editor points out: 'each story belongs somewhere inside the general pattern, yet none of them quite fits; just as individual lives can never be contained or wholly explained by the social and economic realities that circumscribe them'.[48] The return to and re-evaluation of childhood, Liz Heron suggests, may shed light both on the socialisation that leads to a shared oppression as women, *and* on the individual differences that may divide.

Yet to read these evocative, nostalgic accounts is to be struck by the overwhelming similarities – and how similar they seem to my own childhood, which I had imagined as so uniquely estranging. None quite fit the stereotypes; these women come from backgrounds that were slightly odd, they were slight misfits, with parents from disparate class backgrounds, or, in one case, of different races; but all found in academic achievement a way out of the tantalising open prison of childhood. Each account ends with a coda charting subsequent 'success', as Laura Marcus points out in her perceptive discussion of autobiography.[49] These women are now published writers, university teachers, work in the media.

I do not think, as Laura Marcus does, that it is these 'happy endings' that 'flatten out the differences', but rather that these women articulate the ambiguities of a particular calling; for are we not all the female inheritors of that breed which John Gross called 'the man of letters'.[50] In the 20th century it is the woman of letters as much as the man who lives her sense of uniqueness and talent as part of an insecure intelligentsia that makes its living on the margins of the dominant culture. We inhabit a feminised Grub Street that is even further decentred by reason of our gender than was the shabby world of the snobs and scribblers, the hacks and would be geniuses described by Gross and, of course, by George Gissing; indeed, in *The Odd Women*[51] Gissing described the uneasy lives of women who even then were trying to live on their wits.

In *Truth Dare or Promise*, one contribution, by Carolyn Steedman, is an extract from her own autobiographical *Landscape for a Good Woman*.[52] In this, fragments of autobiography centred round her mother are used as a kind of oral history and analytic recall, by means of which she mounts a theoretical critique of some of the stereotypes found in documentary oral and other histories of the working class. The mother of the narrative rejects the matriarchal warmth of the working class 'Mum' celebrated in books such as Richard Hoggart's *The Uses of Literacy*,[53] and instead yearns for the femininity of a 'New Look' outfit, which becomes in Carolyn Steedman's narrative a symbolic representation of women's desire as against the heroic *class* imperatives of that rather sentimentalised working class tradition. As Laura Marcus points out, Carolyn Steedman does not explicitly interrogate the notion of 'identity', yet her book asserts individuality by means of a series of refusals of *identification*: the coldness between mother and daughter; the refusal to share an identity with middle class feminists ('I ... feel the painful familiar sense of exclusion from these stories of middle-class little girlhood and womanhood, envy of those who belong ...'); the stubborn refusal of affirmation.

Yet in this narrative, as in the others, there is a latent assumption of some unquestioned authenticity. It is taken for granted that in claiming their 'right to speak' (that is, to write) these women are uttering what has hitherto been unspoken, and also that it does have status as a 'truth'. Carolyn Steedman goes against the grain, yet also implicitly lays claim to this truth. Her book does, though, question the stereotypes of feminism and of 'class politics' (and indeed this would apply to a politics based on racial oppression as well) in which a one-dimensional awareness of oppression both creates an identity – individual and shared – and absolves the subject from the guilt of an alienated consciousness.

Another group testimony, *Girls Next Door: Lesbian*

Feminist Stories[54] illustrates the impossibility of making a clear distinction between autobiography and fiction, and Alison Hennegan in her introduction comments

> Each of the twenty-two stories printed here has its beginnings in the life lived, not observed, the life known, not imagined ... The overwhelming impulse we can sense at work behind them all remains the same: to try, after so many years of lies told about us and silence imposed upon us, to tell the truth we know as truly as we can.[55]

This could stand as a generous summary of the impulse behind confessional writing in general. Yet truth is not transparent, and in political writing especially there is always a temptation to substitute for it a conventional wisdom which suppresses uncomfortable aspects of truth and relies instead on what eventually become clichés of oppression.

Mirror Writing and *Prisons of Glass* intended (whether they were successful or not is another matter) to problematise the way in which those problems are posed and the feminist 'answers' that are then set up. They also implicitly questioned the very authenticity that is the hallmark of feminist narratives. This includes a questioning of the (fictive) distinction between truth and fiction. Both were autobiographical *and* fictional; just as both aimed *not* to have a 'heroine' with whom the reader could identify. Both aimed to prioritise the inconsistent and fragmentary rather than the coherent. These are in some ways similar to the questions posed at a more sophisticated theoretical – and perhaps at a more arid – level by Carolyn Steedman in terms of narrative and discourse.

Yet it may be that in their very rejection of a transparent authenticity they covertly claim the 'higher' truth of the postmodernist flux of identity and disintegration of experience. And this too can become little more than a modish imperative. Like the compulsion to affirm, this too could become a substitute for a genuinely illuminating exploration of the politics of subjectivity.

I hope, nonetheless, that they can be seen as part of a different tradition that has been established within feminist writing, and not judged within the terms of a confessional tradition they reject. The triumphant ending of the confessional work acts as a form of closure, whereas these others remain open-ended, explore the spaces of uncertainty in the interstices between the 'politically correct' and daily life. And they remind us that, in Doris Lessing's words[56]: 'My life has always been crude, unfinished, raw, tentative ... the raw, unfinished quality in my life was precisely what was valuable in it'.

Notes

[1] Elizabeth Wilson, *Mirror Writing*, Virago, London 1982.

[2] See Marina Warner, *Monuments and Maidens: The Allegory of the Female Form*, Weidenfeld and Nicolson, London 1985.

[3] Elizabeth Wilson, *Prisons of Glass*, Methuen, London 1986.

[4] Lawrence Stone, *The Family, Sex and Marriage in England 1500-1800*, Penguin 1979, p.154.

[5] Charles Rycroft, *Psychoanalysis and Beyond*, Chatto and Windus, London 1985, p.196.

[6] See, for example, Estelle Jelinek (ed) *Women's Autobiography: Essays in Criticism*, Indiana University Press, USA 1980.

[7] Samuel Richardson, *Pamela*, Dent, London 1955 (first published 1740).

[8] John Cleland, *Fanny Hill or Memoirs of a Woman's Pleasure*, Penguin 1985 (first published 1748).

[9] Peter Wagner, 'Introduction' in Cleland, *op cit*, pp.22-23.

[10] Jean-Jacques Rousseau, *The Confessions*, Penguin 1953 (first published 1780).

[11] See Rachel Bowlby, *Just Looking: Consumer Culture in Dreiser, Gissing and Zola*, Methuen, London 1985.

[12] See Sandra Frieden, *Autobiography: Self into Form: German Language Autobiographical Writings of the 1970s*, Verlag Peter Lang, Frankfurt am Main, 1983.

[13] Simone de Beauvoir, *The Second Sex*, Cape, London 1953.

[14] Betty Friedan, *The Feminine Mystique*, Penguin 1963.

[15] See Nicola Beaumann, *A Very Great Tradition: The Woman's Novel 1914-1939*, Virago, London 1983.

[16] Doris Lessing, *The Golden Notebook*, Penguin 1964.

[17] Anja Meulenbelt, *The Shame is Over*, The Women's Press, London 1980.

[18] Verena Stefan, *Shedding*, The Women's Press, London 1980.

[19] Rosamund Lehmann, *Dusty Answer*, Penguin 1982, p. 302 (first published 1927).

[20] Rosalind Coward, 'Cautionary Tales', *New Socialist*, July/August 1984, p. 47.

[21] Alison Fell, *Every Move You Make*, Virago, London 1984.

[22] Catherine Stimpson, *Classnotes*, Avon, New York 1979.

[23] Maureen Brady and Judith McDaniel, 'Lesbians in the Mainstream: Images of Lesbians in Recent Commercial Fiction', *Conditions*, vol 2, no 2, 1980, p.82, 103.

[24] Selwyn R Cudjoe, 'Maya Angelou and the Autobiographical Statement' in Mari Evans (ed), *Black Women Writers*, Pluto, London 1985.

[25] *Ibid*, p.9.

[26] *Ibid*, p.20.

[27] Maya Angelou, *Gather Together in My Name*, Virago, London 1985.

[28] Cudjoe, *op cit*, p.20.

[29] *Ibid*, p.24.

[30] Sondra O'Neale, 'Reconstruction of the Composite Self: New Images of Black Women in Maya Angelou's Continuing Autobiography' in Evans, *op cit*, p.26.

[31] Margaret Walters, 'The Rights and Wrongs of Women: Mary Wollstonecraft, Harriet Martineau, Simone de Beauvoir' in Juliet Mitchell and Ann Oakley (eds), *The Rights and Wrongs of Women*, Penguin 1976.

[32] Mary Evans, *Simone de Beauvoir: A Feminist Mandarin*, Tavistock, London 1985.

[33] Helen Taylor, 'The Cult of the Woman Author', *Women's Review*, no 5, March 1986, p.40.

[34] Richard Dyer, *Stars*, British Film Institute, London 1979, p.37.

[35] Mary Evans, 'A Postscript on de Beauvoir', *New Left Review* no 159, September/October 1986, p.36.

[36] Angela Davis, *Women Race and Class*, The Women's Press, London 1983.

[37] Radclyffe Hall, *The Well of Loneliness*, Virago, London 1982 (first published 1927).

[38] Toril Moi, *Sexual/Textual Politics*, Methuen, London 1985, p.40.

[39] Gertrude Stein, *The Autobiography of Alice B Toklas*, Penguin 1977 (first published 1933).

[40] James E Breslin, 'Gertrude Stein and the Problems of Autobiography', in Jelinek, *op cit*, p.152.

[41] Sheila Rowbotham, *Woman's Consciousness, Man's World*, Penguin, 1973.

[42] *Ibid*, p.33.

[43] Kate Millett, *Sexual Politics*, Rupert Hart Davis, London 1970.

[44] Kate Millett, *The Prostitution Papers*, Paladin, London 1973, p.10.

[45] Kate Millett, *Flying*, Hart Davis McGibbon, London 1975, and *Sita*, Virago, London 1978.

[46] R Curb and N Manahan, *Breaking Silence: Lesbian Nuns on Convent Sexuality*, Colombus Books, New York 1985.

[47] Liz Heron, *Truth Dare or Promise: Girls Growing Up in the Fifties*, Virago, London 1985.

[48] *Ibid*, p.1.

[49] Laura Marcus, ' "Enough About You, Let's Talk About Me": Recent Autobiographical Writing', *New Formations*, No 1, Spring 1987.

[50] John Gross, *The Rise and Fall of the Man of Letters: Aspects of English Literary Life Since 1800*, Weidenfeld and Nicolson, London 1969.

[51] George Gissing, *The Odd Women*, Virago, London 1980, (first published 1983).

[52] Carolyn Steedman, *Landscape for a Good Woman*, Virago, London 1986.

[53] Richard Hoggart, *The Uses of Literacy*, Penguin, 1957.

[54] S Bradshaw and J Hemming (eds), *Girls Next Door: Lesbian Feminist Stories*, The Women's Press, 1985.

[55] Alison Hennegan, 'Introduction' in Bradshaw and Hemming *op cit*, p.1.

[56] Doris Lessing, *op cit*, p.233.

Children of the Night: Vampirism as Homosexuality, Homosexuality as Vampirism

RICHARD DYER

One of the first popular gay stories ever published is a vampire story. By popular I don't mean 'most widely read', which in mass market terms it certainly wasn't, but 'produced by and for gay people themselves'; and by 'gay', I mean to indicate homosexuality as a social identity. A 'gay story' is then one written by someone who experiences their homosexual preferences as defining their personality and/or social role. Such a person was Carl Heinrich Ulrichs, who published his vampire short story 'Manor' in Leipzig in 1885.[1]

Ulrichs was one of the first people to write about and proclaim a gay identity, coming out, as we would say now, to his family in 1862 and thereafter publishing a series of mostly theoretical books on the nature and rights of homosexuals.[2] 'Manor' is set in the Faroe Islands and tells of the love between a youth, Har, and Manor, a seaman; when the latter is killed at sea in a storm, he returns as a spirit and sucks blood at Har's breast; the islanders realise what is happening and drive a stake through Manor's corpse, but Har is so alone without Manor that he wills himself to die; his last wish is that he be laid beside Manor in the grave and that the stake be removed from Manor's corpse – 'And they did what he asked'.

The date of 'Manor' is remarkable, but the choice of the vampire image is less so. The vampire returns time and

47

again in popular gay writing. *Der Eigene*, a gay male magazine published in Berlin by Adolf Brand between 1896 and 1931 contained much vampire imagery in its fiction and at least one complete vampire story.[3] The British 'bisexual' magazine of the early 1970s, *Jeremy*, published in one of its first editions Count Stenbock's 'The True Story of a Vampire', a gay vampire tale first published in 1894. Two of the cult novels in US gay circles in the 1970s and 80s, though not written by a gay man, have been Anne Rice's *Interview with the Vampire*, and *The Vampire Lestat*,[4] in which gay love is an inherent part of the ecstasies of vampirising.

Even when not specifically vampiric, gay writers have often been drawn more generally to the Gothic from early on in the genre's existence, with such notable examples as William Beckford's *Vathek* (1786), Matthew Lewis's *The Monk* (1796) and Mario Vacano's *Mysterien des Welt und Bühnenlebens* (1861). At the other end of the time scale, one of the most successful of the new wave of gay pulp fiction in the 1970s was Vincent Varga's splendid parody, *Gaywick*,[5] and several other gay Gothic novels have been published since then.

From 'Manor' to *The Vampire Lestat*, or from *Vathek* to *Gaywick*, there is a line of vampire or Gothic writing that is predominantly gay produced, or which at any rate forms part of a gay male reading tradition. The situation in relation to lesbianism and vampirism is, as one should expect, different. There is certainly a tradition of lesbian vampires in literature – a listing would probably come up with more titles than with gay male vampires, and with some classier names, including Coleridge and Baudelaire. Yet the overwhelming majority of this lesbian vampire literature was produced by men, notably the influential story by Sheridan LeFanu, 'Carmilla'.[6]

It would of course help my argument if I could now reveal the existence of a tradition of lesbian-produced lesbian vampire fiction, but I can't. There are, however, arguments that point towards the possibility or potential for such a tradition.

To begin with there are two recent uses of the vampire

theme by lesbian writers – Jody Scott's science fiction novel
I, Vampire[7] and Jewelle Gomez' short story 'No Day Too
Long'.[8] In both the female vampire is the heroine and her
vampirising activity is celebrated. *I, Vampire* is about an
affair between the main character, an androgynously
named but definitely female vampire Sterling O'Blivion,
and a genderless creature from outer space (lesbianism
breaks down all gender barriers) who is in disguise as
Virginia Woolf (lesbianism as a definite sexual identity and
tradition). 'No Day Too Long' has the centre vampire
character Gilda resisting her attraction to the younger
woman Effie until she discovers that Effie too is a vampire
'centuries older than she' (p 225) and she has no reason to
run away from her; Gilda is a vampire who lives off
mortals' blood but does not kill them or seek to turn them
into 'a creature of the night like herself' (p 224), so it is
only when she meets another like herself that she can give
her love.

There seems however to be no lesbian-produced lesbian
vampire tradition behind these two tales. There is no
reference to a lesbian vampire novel written by a lesbian in
Jeannette Foster's *Sex Variant Women in Literature*,[9] an
exhaustive survey of the lesbian in literature, nor have I
yet come up with anything from hours of scouring the
shelves of lesbian/gay bookshops, such as Gay's the Word
in London or Giovanni's Room in Philadelphia. Yet it is
hard to believe that *I, Vampire* and 'No Day Too Long'
emerge out of nothing whatsoever. If there are no lesbian
vampire fictions, there is certainly a tradition of lesbian
Gothic, going back at least as far as Djuna Barnes'
Nightwood (1937)[10] and coming up to date with such
enjoyably self-conscious novels as Victoria Ramstetter's
The Marquise and the Novice (1981).[11] This in turn relates to
the general status of Gothic as a 'female' genre, first
developed by women, centering on female protagonists
and exhibiting a strong sense of being addressed to
women.[12] The most famous illustration of the idea that
there is something particularly female-centred about the
Gothic is of course Jane Austen's *Northanger Abbey*, first
published in 1818, which pokes fun at its heroine's naive

fascination in things Gothic as culled from her extensive reading.

It is perhaps worth pointing out the form of the argument in the previous paragraph, since it diverges so markedly from one that could be made about male Gothic literature. Essentially I argued – as a matter of course, when I first wrote it down – that you could argue for there being something 'lesbian' about vampire literature by pointing to the fact not only of lesbian Gothic but also the tradition of female Gothic in general. In other words, I argued the lesbian potential of the genre from its relevance to women in general, and not just lesbian women. You could not make the same sort of case in relation to gay men. Whereas lesbian fiction and culture can often be seen as an extension of female literary and cultural traditions, gay male traditions are often at odds with male fiction and culture. Lesbian Gothic extends forms and feelings well developed within women's writing as a whole;[13] whereas gay Gothic is precisely not like men's writing – indeed, Gothic fiction, when it is not written by women, has been predominantly the product of gay men and/or men who otherwise, as David Punter puts it, 'display in their works and in their lives a tangential relation to socialised masculine norms ...'.[14] Thus it may be that lesbian vampires/lesbian Gothic is a continuation of aspects of female culture, whereas gay vampires/gay Gothic is a deviation from male culture.

The lesbian/female Gothic tradition suggests a context for contemporary lesbian vampire writing; there is also the possibility of a lesbian reading of vampire images produced by men, as Bonnie Zimmerman's article on the lesbian vampire film suggests. Such a reading may even find something rather progressive in the image:

> The myth of the lesbian vampire ... carries in it the potentiality for a feminist revision of meaning ... sexual attraction between women can threaten the authority of a male-dominated society. The lesbian vampire [story] can lend itself to an even more extreme reading: that in turning to each other, women triumph over and destroy men themselves.[15]

The recent short British film *The Mark of Lilith*[16] explores some of these feminist possibilities.

In addition to specific traditions of gay and lesbian vampire fictions, there is at a broader level a fit between the values and feelings explored and produced by the vampire genre and the values and feelings of emergent lesbian and gay male identities in the 19th and 20th centuries. What has been imagined through the vampire image is of a piece with how people have thought and felt about lesbians and gay men – how others have thought and felt about us, and how we have thought and felt about ourselves. Let me illustrate this here from a rather negative example.

Lillian Faderman[17] suggests that there is a virtual sub-genre of lesbian vampire novels in the early part of the 20th century, citing such examples as *Regiment of Women* (1915) by Winifred Ashton (under the pseudonym of Clemence Dane), *White Ladies* (1935) by Francis Brett Young and *Trio* (1943) by Dorothy Baker. These are not vampire novels in the strictest sense of the term – there is no blood-sucking, no notions of being 'un-dead', none of the paraphernalia of the popular vampire tales. But the imagery describing the lesbian relationships in these novels is drawn from vampirism. In *Regiment of Women* the effect on Alwynne of her relationship with Clare (the headteacher of the school where she works) is noted by Elsbeth, Alwynne's aunt:

> So thin – she's growing so dreadfully thin. Her neck! You should see her neck – salt-cellars, literally! And she had such a beautiful neck! ... And so white and listless![18]

The effect of lesbianism is the same as the effect of vampirism in the classic vampire tales – loss of weight, loss of blood, loss of energy. Perhaps even more striking here is the effect on the victim's neck – no bite marks, yet still the focus of anxious attention. When Alwynne is 'saved' by taking a holiday away from Clare and meeting a young man, her symptoms disappear; on her return she has 'grown *rosy* and cheerful, affectionate and satisfyingly garrulous' (p 278, my emphasis). Even more devastatingly vampiric is the effect Clare has on one of her pupils, Louise, who kills herself, leaving behind in one of her school essays a chilling description of being 'pressed to death' by a slab of stone – ostensibly an account of medieval torture, the writing swiftly becomes personalised until she seems to be writing of her morbid fantasies of death:

> ... and all the time the stone is sinking – sinking ... And perhaps you go to sleep at last ... Perhaps you dream. You dream you are free and people love you, and you have done nothing wrong and you are frightfully happy, and the one you love most kisses your forehead. But then the kiss grows so cold that you shrink away, only you cannot, and it presses you harder and harder, and you wake up and it is the stone. It is the sinking stone that is pressing you, pressing you, pressing you to death ...[19]

The kiss stolen in the victim's sleep, a kiss s/he desires until s/he realises it is literally the kiss of death – this is classic vampire imagery, and in the context it is clear that 'the one you love most' is, for Louise, Clare.

Even where the language of the writing does not so explicitly evoke vampirism, the nature of the relationships in the novels Faderman discusses is always one in which a stronger woman dominates and draws the life out of a weaker (and often younger) woman. Faderman's discussion is part of a wider account of a shift in the social definition of intense relationships between women. Where earlier periods had conceived of 'romantic friendships' between women (which might or might not have involved sexual relations), by the early 20th century the medical and psychological profession had started to think of such relationships in terms of 'lesbianism', as, in other words, defined by the sexual element. Faderman sees this as springing from men's desire to prohibit the possibility of women forming important attachments to each other separate from and even over against their attachments to men. The notion of 'lesbianism', seen as a sickness, was used to discredit both romantic friendship between women and the growth of women's political and educational independence. Thus there is a fit between the general associations of the vampire tale and the way in which friendships between women were being pathologised in the period.

As I indicated, Faderman's examples are negative instances of the general point I wish to make about the fit between vampire imagery and lesbian/gay identities. Quite apart from misgivings I may have about Faderman's distaste for lesbian identities and her assumption that such identities are necessarily male imposed, I want here to discuss *both* the negative and the positive ways in which thinking and feeling about being lesbian/gay has been expressed, by writers and readers, in vampire imagery.

There is a clear tradition of gay male vampire writing and reading, and a rather more ambivalent lesbian tradition. Why should the vampire image have drawn gay/lesbian attention?

It is possible to suggest historically specific reasons for the association of homosexuality and vampirism. Vampires are classically aristocrats and much of the development of a public face for homosexuality and/or decadent sexuality was at the hands of aristocrats – de Sade, Byron – or writers posing as aristocrats – Lautréamont, Wilde. The female character whose potential vampirism is most threatening in *Dracula*, Mina, is associated with the emergent 'New Woman' in Victorian society, financially and maritally independent.[20] From New Woman to lesbian is but a step in the ideology of the day, leading to the vampiric lesbianism discussed by Faderman. In the German gay writings up to the 1930s vampirism is the consummation of love with a dead young man, who may represent the lost perfect friendship extolled by the youth movements and/or the loved one lost in the slaughter of the First World War, common themes in the writing of the period. Such historically precise connections certainly account for particular inflections of gay/lesbian vampire images, but it is the wider metaphorical possibilities of the vampire that account for its longer hold in lesbian/gay terms.

The image of the vampire has been used to mean many things – such is the nature of popular cultural symbolism. The vampire has represented the weight of the past as it lays on the present, or the way the rich live off the poor, or the threat of an unresolved and unpeaceful death, or the baneful influence of Europe on American culture, or an alternative life-style as it threatens the established order, or the way the listless white race leeches off the vigour of the black races. The vampire has been used to articulate all such meanings and more,[21] yet the sexual symbolism of the vampire does seem the most obvious, and many of the other meanings are articulated through the sexual meanings.

The sexuality of the vampire image is obvious if one compares the vampire to two of her/his close relations, as it were – the zombie and the werewolf. The zombie, like the vampire, is 'un-dead', a human being who has died but nonetheless still leads, unlike the vampire, a mindless existence. Zombies are kept alive in some versions under the spell of voodoo, in others by a purely instinctive drive to savage and eat human flesh. The werewolf, like the vampire, operates only at night and, like the zombie, savages the humans whose flesh he[22] consumes. All three can articulate notions of sexuality. Robin Wood, and a number of other writers on the horror film, have suggested, adapting Freudian ideas, that all 'monsters' in some measure represent the hideous and terrifying form that sexual energies take when they 'return' from being socially and culturally repressed.[23] Yet the vampire seems especially to represent sexuality, for his/her interest in humans is not purely instinctual, and s/he does not characteristically savage them – s/he bites them, with a bite just as often described as a kiss.

The vampire characteristically sinks his/her teeth into the neck of his/her victim and sucks the blood out. You don't *have* to read this as a sexual image, but an awful lot suggests that you should. Even when the writing does not seem to emphasise the sexual, the act itself is so like a sexual act that it seems almost perverse not to see it as one. Biting itself is after all part of the repertoire of sexual acts; call it a kiss, and, when it is as deep a kiss as this, it is a sexual act; it is then by extension obviously analogous to other forms of oral sex acts, all of which (fellatio, cunnilingus, rimming) importantly involve contact not only with orifices but with body fluids as well. Moreover, it is not just what the vampire does that makes it so readable in sexual terms but the social space that it occupies. The act of vampirism takes place in private, at night, most archetypally in a bedroom – the same space which our society accords to the sex act.

That vampirism has been thought of in sexual terms is evident when one starts to look at how it is in fact described. *Dracula* contains passages that are pretty well pornographic in their detailing of the experience of being vampirised:

> The fair girl went on her knees and bent over me, fairly gloating. There was a deliberate voluptuousness which was both thrilling and repulsive, and as she arched her neck she actually licked her lips like an animal, till I could see in the moonlight the moisture shining on the scarlet lips and on the red tongue as it lapped the white sharp teeth ... Then ... I could feel the soft, shivering touch of the lips on the supersensitive skin of my throat, and the hard dents of two sharp teeth, just touching and pausing there. I closed my eyes in a languorous ecstasy and waited – waited with beating heart.[24]

Compare this ecstasy with that evoked 80 years later by Anne Rice in *Interview with the Vampire*, where it is possible to make more explicit genital reference but which is in other respects only building on the delicious perversity of the voluptuousness already evoked so clearly in Stoker. Here the vampire is the narrator and, like his 'victim' (surely 'lover'?), is male:

'Never had I felt this, never had I experienced it, this yielding of a conscious mortal. But before I could push him away for his own sake, I saw the bluish bruise on his tender neck. He was offering it to me. He was pressing the length of his body against me now, and I felt the hard strength of his sex beneath his clothes pressing against my leg. A wretched gasp escaped my lips, but he bent close, his lips on what must have been so cold, so lifeless for him; and I sank my teeth into his skin, my body rigid, that hard sex driving against me, and I lifted him in passion off the floor. Wave after wave of his beating heart passed into me as, weightless, I rocked with him, devouring him, his ecstasy, his conscious pleasure.'[25]

The vampire idea lends itself to a sexual reading and is even, in Rosemary Jackson's words, 'perhaps the highest symbolic representation of eroticism'.[26] It has articulated particular conceptions of sexuality (in Jackson, psychoanalytic ones). I want to go through some of these now, indicating both how they relate to general ideas about sexuality and how they are particularly amenable to gay/lesbian interpretations. I shall be making reference to explicitly lesbian and gay vampire fictions, and also to heterosexual fictions where nonetheless much of the form of the vampirism/sexuality is homologous with the social constructions of lesbian and gay sexuality.

To begin with, the physical space where the act of vampirism/sex takes place is of course also a symbolic, psychological space, namely the realm of the private. It is at night when we are alone in our beds that the vampire classically comes to call, when we are by ourselves and as we commonly think when we are most ourselves. Equally, it is one of the contentions of the history of sexuality developed by Michel Foucault,[27] Jeffrey Weeks[28] and others, that we live in an age which considers the sexual to be both the most private of things and the realm of life in which we are most ourselves.

The privacy of the sexual is embodied in one of the set-pieces of the vampire tale – the heroine left by herself at night, the vampire at the window tapping to come in. Yet as so often with popular genre conventions, this set-piece is also endlessly being reversed, departed from. Very often, it is not the privatised experience of the act of vampirism that is given us, but those thrilling moments when the privacy is violated. Voyeurism, the act of seeing without being seen, is a central narrative device in the vampire story; it is the means by which the hero discovers the vampirism of the vampire and the sensation lies not only in the lurid description of fangs dripping with blood and swooning victims their clothes all awry, but also in that sense of violating a moment of private physical consummation, violating its privacy by looking at it.

Voyeurism is one of the vampire tale's perverse disruptions of the construction of the sexual as private and is central to the genre. Characteristically, it is Anne Rice who further twists the pleasures of perversity by introducing exhibitionism, actively displaying sexuality to the view. In *Interview with the Vampire*, she depicts a Théâtre des Vampires in 19th century Paris. Louis, the narrator of the book (the interviewee of the title), visits the show and sees performed a strange, ritualistic play in which a young woman is sucked to death by a band of vampires. The sensuality of the scene is emphasised by the language and by the emphasis on the way the audience leans forward to *see* the moment of ravishment. They are relishing the enactment of the decadent idea of vampirism; but Louis, and therefore the reader, knows these vampires are no actors and the woman's sacrifice no mere performance. So not only do we pick up on the frisson of the jaded Paris audience, but we have the extra thrill of knowing that we, through Louis, are really seeing a fatal act of vampirism.

There is nothing inherently gay or lesbian in the ideas of privacy, voyeurism and exhibitionism. Yet homosexual desire, like other forbidden sexual desires, may well find expression, as a matter of necessity rather than exquisite choice, in privacy and voyeurism. The sense that being lesbian/gay is something one must keep to oneself certainly accords with an idea of the authenticity of private sexuality, but it is also something one had better keep private if one is not to lose job, family, friends and so on. Furtive looking may be the most one dare do. In this

context, exhibitionism may take on a special voluptuousness, emerging from the privacy of the closet in the most
extravagant act of going public.

Vampirism is not merely, like all our sexuality, private, it
is also secret. It is something to be hidden, to be done
without anyone knowing. The narrative structure of the
vampire tale frequently consists of two parts – the first
leading up to the discovery of the vampire's hidden
nature, the second concerned with his/her destruction. It
is this first part that I want to consider here.

In most vampire tales, the fact that a character is a
vampire is only gradually discovered – it is a secret that has
to be discovered. The analogy with homosexuality as a
secret erotic practice works in two contradictory ways. On
the one hand, the point about sexual orientation is that it
doesn't 'show', you can't tell who is and who isn't just by
looking; but on the other hand, there is also a widespread
discourse that there *are* tell-tale signs that someone 'is'.
The vampire myth reproduces this double view in its very
structures of suspense.

On the one hand, much of the suspense of the story is
about 'finding out'. There are strange goings-on, people
dying of a mysterious plague, characters feeling unac-
countably weak after a deep night's sleep, noticing odd
scratches or a pair of little holes at their neck – what can it
all mean? The nature of this suspense may vary for the
reader. It may be a genuine mystery to us, so that the
discovery of what has caused all this – vampires – and/or
who (which already known character) has caused it, comes
as a satisfying moment of revelation akin to the pleasures
of the whodunnit. However, it is probably the case that
one seldom reads a vampire story without knowing that
that is what it is. This is especially true since the
publication of *Dracula* and even more so when you are
reading any of the numerous collections of vampire tales.
The first readers of 'Carmilla' may have had the shock of
discovery that Carmilla is a vampire (compounded by the
fact that she is lesbian) but few people reading it to-day are
likely to be unforearmed. Rather what we enjoy is knowing
that plagues, fatigues, scratches and holes spell vampire,

and the suspense that that affords us: when will s/he find out what we already know and will it be in time (before being vampirised, or else dying)? A special inflection here lies in the use of first person narrators, so that all we get is the narrator's perceptions and yet we know, as old hands at the genre, what those perceptions mean. So the sense of menace, as the narrator rubs shoulders with the person we know is a vampire, is greater for us than her/him – we know better.

Such reader-text relations offer specific pleasures to gay/lesbian readers. Much of the suspense of a life lived in the closet is, precisely, will they find out? An obvious way to read a vampire story is self-oppressively, in the sense of siding with the narrator (whether s/he is the main character or not) and investing energy in the hope that s/he will be saved from the knowledge of vampirism (homosexuality). Maybe that is how we have often read it. But there are other ways. One is to identify with the vampire in some sort, despite the narrative position, and to enjoy the ignorance of the main character(s). What fools these mortals be. The structure whereby we the reader know more than the protagonist (heightened in first person narration) is delicious, and turns what is perilous in a closeted lesbian/gay life (knowing something dreadful about us they don't) into something flattering, for it makes one superior. Another enjoyable way of positioning oneself in this text-reader relation is in thrilling to the extraordinary power credited to the vampire, transcendant powers of seduction, s/he can have anyone s/he wants, it seems. Most lesbians and gay men experience exactly the opposite, certainly outside of the gay scene, certainly up until very recently. Even though the vampire is invariably killed off at the end (except in recent examples), how splendid to know what a threat our secret is to them!

The structure of the narration reinforces the idea that you can't tell who is and isn't, but the descriptive language often suggests the opposing discourse, that you can indeed spot a queer. It is not that they often come on with all the accoutrements of the screen vampires of Lugosi, Lee et al; perhaps only Dracula and a few very close to him are described like that. What there are instead are give-away aspects of character. Count Vardalek, for instance, in 'The True Story of a Vampire' is tall and fair with an attractive smile. Nothing very vampiric about this, as the narrator herself notes. But along with it is he is also 'refined', with an 'intense sadness of the expression of the eyes'; he looks 'worn and wearied'; above all, he is 'very pale'.[29] There is even less of the vampire about Carmilla, except that – and it is the give-away to alert readers – 'her movements were languid – *very* languid – indeed'.[30]

Not only has it been common to try to indicate that you can always tell a queer/lessie if you know how (indeed, this is one of the functions of gay stereotypes[31]) but very often the vocabulary of queer spotting has been the languid, worn, sad, refined paleness of vampire imagery. This is what makes the lesbianism of the books discussed by Faderman vampiric; it is what used to tell me, in the 1950s and 60s, that a book had a gay theme – if it was called *Women in the Shadows*, *Twilight Men*, *Desire in the Shadows* then it had to be about queers. This imagery derives in part from the idea of decadence, people who do not go out into public life, whose complexions are not weathered, who are always indoors or in the shade. It may also relate to the idea that lesbians and gay men are not 'real' women and 'real' men, we have not got the blood (with its very different gender associations) of normal human beings.

The ideas of privacy and secrecy also suggest the idea of a double life – s/he looks normal, but underneath s/he's a vampire/queer. This simple structure is often given complex inflections. At the end of 'Carmilla' the narrator, Laura, recalls the two faces of vampire Carmilla: 'sometimes the playful, languid, beautiful, girl; sometimes the writhing fiend I saw in the ruined church'.[32] Part of the fascination of the story however lies in the way these two aspects of Carmilla's personality alternate, merge and interact. Perhaps they are less separate than Laura, ten years later, likes to think, for it is possible that her adolescent crush on Carmilla was not only because of the latter's languidness ... In 'The Beautiful Vampire'[33] the priest hero Romuald has succumbed to the vampiric caresses of Clarimonde who visits him and

> From that night onward my nature was in some way doubled; there was within me two men, neither of whom knew the other. Sometimes I thought I was a priest who dreamed every night he was a nobleman, sometimes I was a nobleman who dreamed that he was a priest.[34]

Not only does the act of vampirism release the character's sexuality, and not only is the latter equated with nobility and chastity with the priesthood, but a fascinating ambivalence remains, since both the sexual and chaste sides of himself dream of being the other.

The classic metaphoric Gothic statement of the idea of the gay male double life is Wilde's *The Portrait of Dorian Gray*, which has fixed an image of the gay man as a sparkling, agreeable surface masking a hidden depravity, brilliant charm concealing a corrupt and sordid sexuality. Dorian Gray in Wilde's novel is not a vampire, but in *The Amplified Journal of D.G.* (serialised anonymously in the magazine *Mandate*, a sort of gay equivalent of *Playboy*) he is.[35] In the second diary entry (published October 1986), the narrator explains that he has given himself the name Dorian Gray, because that is the name Wilde gave the character for which the narrator was the original inspiration. Thus 'D.G.' suggests that Dorian Gray, the archetype of gay male existence, is a fundamentally vampiric creation.

Vampirism is private and secret, and may therefore be the terrible reality of the inner self, but in another sense it is beyond the self because it is beyond the individual's will and control. This is true for vampire and victim alike. The vampire is driven on by the absolute necessity for blood to stay 'alive', s/he can't help herself; the victim is either asleep or mesmerised by the vampire's power or charm, so that s/he has no responsibility for surrendering to her/his kiss.

The gay resonances are even stronger here. One of the

most important – and, it must be said, effective – ways in
which homosexuality has been justified and defended in
the 20th century is through the argument that 'we/they
can't help it'. Much of the feel of apologia for homosexuality, whether written by gay men and lesbians themselves or
by others, has been a mix of distaste for homosexuality with
a recognition that it cannot be resisted – 'I don't know why I
want to do these disgusting things, but I do and can't stop
myself and there's no real harm in it'.

But the point about uncontrollability is more interesting
than that. There is, as indicated above, an active and a
passive form to this lack of control, but from this it does not
follow that to be active is correlated with being male or
being passive with female. Even *Dracula*, while it gives us the
typical   lady-asleep-with-vampire-at-her-neck set-pieces,
also gives us the delirium of the pleasures of male passivity.

> I closed my eyes in a languorous ecstasy and waited – waited
> with beating heart.[36]

Alas, the Count interrupts the fulfilment of Jonathan
Harker's languor, and his own no doubt even more
delicately soft-yet-hard treatment of Jonathan's recum-
bent person is concealed in the gap between two
chapters.[37] Equally enthralled by the pleasures of passivity
is Romuald in 'The Beautiful Vampire' and here the
language of male sexuality is applied to what the woman
does, first at the moment of seduction:

> the coolness of Clarimonde's hand *penetrated* mine, and I felt
> voluptuous shivers run all over my body.[38]

and later when she holds sway over him and the phallic
imagery (the needle, the prick, the man lying back and
enjoying it) is clear enough for the most unconvinced
Freudian:

When she felt sure that I was asleep, she bared my arm and drew a golden pin from her hair; then she began to murmur in a low voice:

'One drop, just one little red drop, a ruby on the point of my needle! ... Ah! poor love! your beautiful blood, such a vivid crimson, I am going to drink it! Sleep, my only treasure; sleep, my god, my child ... Ah! what a lovely arm! how round it is! how white it is! I shall never dare to prick that pretty blue vein.'[39]

But of course she does dare, to everyone's (her, his, our) satisfaction. Indeed her threat not to dare to prick him can be seen as a classic foreplay tease of the passive lover; while her love language evokes her as both adoringly subservient woman ('my god') *and* warmly encompassing mother ('my child') even while in fact being phallic woman.

The pleasures of passivity for men are then frequently evoked in vampire fiction; the pleasures of activity for women less so. We have images of sexually/vampirically active women, and no doubt these can be identified with, but the point-of-view is nearly always the man's. This is partly because, as discussed below, until recently very few vampire stories are told from the point of view of the vampire anyway, but only from that of the victim or onlooker. So although we have images of an active female sexuality, this is more often seen in terms of its threat/treat for the man. It is not until Jody Scott's *I, Vampire* that we get the pleasures of active female desire, and then with a vengeance:

And then the thrill of victory forever new, the ritualized ecstasy as I master the unconscious victim and at long last that slow, marvellous caress on the tongue as the Ruby slips down my throat ...[40]

Again, male passivity and female activity, and slipping between the two, does not have to be an expression of lesbian/gay sexuality, but there is no doubt that the felt inevitability, or propriety, of the usual equation in heterosexual relations goes to the wall in homosexual ones. It is not very profitable to talk in terms of active and

passive in relation to oral sex, which is, after mutual mastur-
bation, the commonest form of lesbian and gay sexual
practice. It is also the most obvious sexual reference point
of vampirism. Though there is often much gender role-
playing, even to the point of exaggeration, in gay and
lesbian relationships, this correlates unpredictably with
who does what in bed, who is really strongest in the
relationship. The play of gender role, sexual position,
active/passive is part of the structure of vampirism and
lesbian/gay sexuality alike – unlike heterosexuality (at least
at the level of representation) such play is the rule not the
exception.

The ideas in vampire fiction of what sexuality is like –
privacy, secrecy, uncontrollability, active/passive – have a
complex relationship to the place of sexuality within the
social order. Until the 1960s – and, really still today –
sexuality was approved within marriage. Vampirism takes
place outside of marriage. Marriage is the social institution
of the privacy of sexuality – the vampire violates it, tapping
at the window to get in, providing sexual scenes for the
narrator to witness. Marriage contains female sexuality –
hence the horror of the female vampire, walking the streets
at night in search of sex. Men are allowed to walk those
streets for that purpose, hence the ambivalence of the male
vampire, the fulfilment of the importunate nature of male
sexuality, dangerous, horrible, but also taken to be what
men, alas, are. Finally marriage restricts sexuality to heterosexuality – vampirism is the alternative, dreaded and
desired in equal measure.

I have so far been trying to indicate why vampirism is so
easy to read as an image of gay/lesbian sexuality and experience. What interests me finally is the way this potential for
gay/lesbian meaning also articulates evaluations of homosexuality. In all vampire fiction, vampirism can be taken to
evoke the thrill of a forbidden sexuality, but whereas earlier
examples also express horror and revulsion, later examples
turn this on its head and celebrate.

One way we might note this shift in emphasis is in the narrator. In most vampire tales up to the 1970s, the narrator is not her or himself a vampire. Either we have the convention of the omniscient narrator telling what befell a group of people; or we have personal testimony (multiple in the case of *Dracula*) about being involved in a case of vampirism as victim, observer or rescuer. But in no case does the vampire tell his/her own story. Although there may be earlier examples, the most striking example of a shift to the vampire as narrator of his/her own tale is *Interview with the Vampire*, and the very remarkableness of this shift is signalled by the use of the rather elaborate device of having the vampire interviewed. The book starts with an omniscient narrator describing the scene: 'the boy', a magazine reporter, and the vampire together in a room in New Orleans, with the boy eliciting the vampire's story from him. Most of the book consists of the first person narration of the life of Louis, the vampire, but every paragraph opens with double inverted commas to remind us of the interview situation and there are occasional interruptions from the boy, putting questions, asking Louis to stop while he changes the cassette. This device constantly reminds us of the fact that a vampire is speaking for himself. By the time of the sequel, *The Vampire Lestat*, (1985) there is no need for such signalling and we get a straightforward first-person vampire's account of his life. Likewise Jody Scott's *I, Vampire* launches straight into first person vampire narrative. Interestingly some later chapters deal with non-vampire characters in a third person narration. It is not clear whether this is meant to be the words of the hero, Sterling O'Blivion, but in any case it is striking that whereas the vampire speaks for herself, 'normals' are left to be described in the third person from without.

This shift in the position of the narrator *vis-à-vis* vampirism is surely analogous with the shift, and insistence upon it, from lesbians and gay men as persons who are spoken about to persons who speak for themselves. It is also a shift from disgust to delight. Compare the two 'pornographic' quotations above, from

Dracula and *Interview with the Vampire*. In *Dracula* the act is revolting – thrilling but 'repulsive', animalistic, with 'churning' sounds and flesh tingling. When later Jonathan discovers the Count, his vampiric lust satisfied, he describes him 'gorged with blood' laying 'like a filthy leech, exhausted with his repletion'. Louis *and* his 'victim', on the other hand, are both clearly transported by their quite explicitly sexual vampiric union – they experience 'passion', 'ecstasy', 'pleasure'; repeated references to hardness and rigidity indicate male sexual pleasure; and there is even an aesthetising of the experience in the way 'the boy' 'offers' Louis 'the bluish bruise on his tender neck'.

The earlier vampire fictions are not written in the first person, but of course this does not mean that gay men and lesbians may not have identified with the negative image of a disgusting, uncontrollable, forbidden vampire lust. In his 1984 novel, *Why We Never Dance the Charleston*, Harlan Greene describes the lives of a group of young gay men in Charleston in the 1920s. He returns repeatedly to vampire imagery to express how they felt about themselves and being gay:

> I was condemned like a vampire ... to eternal darkness. I was nauseatingly white and sluglike; I was a repulsive moonlit thing that crawled out from under a rock and in to the evening. In a word, I was queer.[41]

Early gay vampire fiction does not in fact express quite such self-loathing as this. In 'Vampir' by Julius Neuss (published in *Der Eigene* in 1922), the vampire Morsa, dark, cadaverous and 'feminine' represents the threat/ promise of adventure and pleasure for Adolf, fair, youthful and muscular. In the end Morsa overcomes Adolf's resistance, the feminine overcoming the muscular, in a sequence of intense moral ambiguity but erotic certainty. Other early tales express a sorrowful sympathy for the 'curse' of being a vampire/queer. 'The True Story of a Vampire' is suffused with melancholy. Count

Vardalek wishes he did not have to vampirise the boy
Gabriel – he says to him:

> 'My darling, I fain would spare thee: but thy life is my life,
> and I must live, I who would rather die. Will God not have *any*
> mercy on me? Oh! oh! life; oh, the torture of life!'[42]

Vardalek's tragedy is that he wants to die but cannot.
Elsewhere vampirism represents the promise of death as a
release from the confines of normal society and the very
form of the consummation of gay love. Har's death in
'Manor' provides a gay happy ending to the story,
becoming 'un-dead' is to become one's true sexual nature.

There is a potential contradiction in the 'positive' use of
the vampire in gay/lesbian fiction. Classically vampires do
not vampirise each other. What will Har and Manor 'do'
now they are both un-dead? The transcendant reunion
that ends the tale leaves this question unasked and,
besides, transcendant friendship was the ostensible goal of
much German gay culture of the period. For later writers
it has been an interesting problem. Vampirism can now be
celebrated as the most exquisite form of sexual pleasuring,
yet it remains outside of ideal sexual relationships. The
different ways of handling this in contemporary lesbian
and gay vampire fiction relate to different conceptions of
what it is to be homosexual within both the lesbian and gay
communities.

One approach is to play down the erotic overtones of
vampirising. In Gomez's 'No Day Too Long', vampirism is
a sign of Gilda's difference, an intensification of her
lesbianism. She was a runaway slave who killed a white
man who'd tracked her down and was made into a
vampire by a woman who found her – her vampirism
relates to an heroic, Amazonian past and separates her
from the mortal lesbians with whom she works as a
night-club singer. Vampirism here is a metaphor for
lesbianism as something more than a sexual preference, a
different way of grasping the essence of womanhood, with
the resonance of the black feminist concept of
'womanism'.[43] The act of vampirising in 'No Day Too

Long' is merely the way Gilda survives; and yet being a vampire does give her character a powerful erotic charge. The point of the narrative is Gilda's happiness at finding someone else like herself. Gilda and Effie, both vampires, end up in each other's arms but not at each other's throats.

Other examples retain the eroticism of vampirism and yet distinguish it from love. In *I, Vampire* Sterling's sexy vampirising is kept distinct from her feeling for her loved one, Benaroya:

> Sterling was deeply, sincerely in love for the first time in her life. But she couldn't even extol her loved one's eyes, lips, hair, and so on; because it was not a body she loved, but a person.[44]

This body/person split is explicable within the narrative, because Benaroya is an alien who has merely assumed the body of Virginia Woolf for its visit to Earth – but the very choice of this device permits a traditional moral dualism for which the relish with which vampirising is described in the book does not prepare you. Anne Rice's two vampire novels dwell at length on the eroticism of vampirism, but they too distinguish it from relationships. In *Interview with the Vampire* there is a pervading sense of loneliness, the endless pursuit of sexual/vampiric ecstasy without romantic fulfillment. Louis hates the other main vampire character in the book, Lestat, the man who made him a vampire. The sequel is Lestat's own story and contains more than one fulfilling gay love affair, but these are sexual without being vampiric. Both partners go on vampirising. The genre requires this, of course, it is how vampires 'live', but, as it retains its erotic charge, it also corresponds to the widespread model of gay male coupledom where a stable central relationship and continued cruising and promiscuity are not held to be incompatible.

AIDS of course has appeared to challenge that model and it might seem too that it spelt the end of 'positive' gay vampire fiction, with body fluids and blood so central to both vampirism and the passing on of AIDS. Yet *The*

Amplified Journal of D.G. (of which as I write only four
'entries' have been published) suggests a different way of
feeling the relationship between AIDS and sexuality.
Dorian, the vampire narrator/hero, cruises New York, a
city that is dying:

> They are renouncing it, they who have kept me company
> since my reawakening from the Long Sleep. Something
> beautiful is dying, and only I will mourn it. Others weep for
> those who pass. I alone weep for what is passing.[45]

The reference is clearly to the decline of gay nightlife with
the coming of AIDS – but the importance is that the writer
continues to affirm that life, to mourn its passing more
than the deaths it has supposedly 'caused'. He rejects too
the antiseptic notions of sexuality with which ideas of 'safe
sex' resonate:

> ... at the notion of 'safe sex' I am bound to laugh. Sex – all sex
> – is dangerous. Between strangers, friends, lovers; between
> husband and wife; in groups, alone. Sex is exquisitely
> dangerous – to the soul, always; to the body, sometimes, if
> your blood should be invaded, or if you and your partner
> should choose to play medieval games before first mastering
> the rules, or if dark misfortune should put you in the arms of
> the wrong alluring stranger.[46]

This is a familiar gay voice – it is the voice of that part of
the gay liberation movement which set itself against
respectability and fitting in, against monogamy and passing
for straight; it is the voice many hear in Genet, and others
of the *poètes maudits*, where depravity and degradation are
validated; it is the voice that prizes gayness as outlawry and
living on the edge. Through the vampire image it pushes
at the boundaries of sexual ecstasy. Even sado-masochism,
often presented as the very frontier of sexual outlawry, is
seen by Dorian as mere theatre, without the true ecstasy of
vampirism. When Dorian, in the first entry, picks up a
man who fancies an s/m scene, the man loses his nerve
when Dorian gets into real (vampiric) sadism. As
elsewhere in the writing, Dorian addresses the reader as

the ideal lover he is looking for; here he compares him, this reader, with the man he has picked up:

> He trembles against me. He sobs on my shoulder. He is not wearing his fear well. There is not a tatter of doubt left in me: He is not you. You would be afraid, yes; but your fear would be thrilling. And you would know how to ride it.[47]

Thus the writer enlists the reader in the fantasy of homosexual outlawry; defiantly he asks us to feel still the thrill of the dangers of sex just at the point when the danger of those thrills seems to have become too great.

The variations in the use of vampirism as homosexuality in contemporary lesbian and gay fiction do not exhaust the range of ways in which lesbians and gay men inhabit their sexuality, but they do indicate that there is life in the metaphor yet. Or rather that it remains un-dead. In all cases vampirism represents something about homosexual desire that remains stubbornly marginal, unruly, fascinating and indispensable – the blood remains, as it was for Dracula, 'the life'. But also in all cases homosexuality is the basis for the most intense, even transcendant romantic relationships. The difference lies in whether this is constructed as something distinct from (blood) lust (Gomez, Scott, Rice) or is to be plucked from the very heart of lust ('D.G.')

Notes

[1] It was reprinted many times thereafter and is now available in Joachim S Hohmann (ed), *Enstellte Engel*, Fisher, Frankfurt am Main 1983, pp.271-278.

[2] His works were known collectively as *Forschungen über das Räthsel der mannmännlichen Liebe* (Researches on the Riddle of Love Between Men). See James D Steakley, *The Homosexual Emancipation Movement in Germany*, Arno Press, New York 1975.

[3] See Hohmann (ed), *Der Eigene. Ein Querschnitt durch die erste Homosexuellenzeitschrift der Welt*, Foerster, Frankfurt/Berlin 1981.

[4] Anne Rice, *Interview with the Vampire*, Futura, London 1977. *The Vampire Lestat*, Knopf, New York 1985.

[5] Vincent Varga, *Gaywick*, Avon Books, New York 1980.

[6] Sheridan Lefanu, 'Carmilla', *In a Glass Darkly*, Eveleigh, Nash and Grayson (first published 1872).

[7] Jody Scott, *I Vampire*, Ace Science Fiction, New York 1984.

[8] Jewelle Gomez, 'No Day Too Long', in Elly Bukin (ed) *Lesbian Fiction*, Persephone, Watertown (Mass) 1981.

[9] Jeanette Foster, *Sex Variant Women in Literature*, Naiad, Tallahassee 1985.

[10] Djuna Barnes, *Nightwood*, Harcourt, Brace and Co, New York 1937.

[11] Victoria Ramstetter, *The Marquise and the Novice*, Naiad, Tallahassee 1981.

[12] Tania Modleski, *Loving with a Vengeance*, Methuen, New York 1984 (first published 1982), pp.59-84.

[13] Ellen Moers, *Literary Women*, The Women's Press, London 1978, pp.90-110.

[14] David Punter, *The Literature of Terror*, Longman, London 1980, p.411.

[15] Bonnie Zimmerman, 'Lesbian Vampires', *Jump Cut* no 24/25, March 1981, pp.23-24.

[16] *The Mark of Lilith* (GB 1986, directed by Bruna Fionda, Polly Gladwin and Isiling Mack-Nataf; distributed in UK by Circles).

[17] Lillian Faderman, *Surpassing the Love of Men*, Morrow, New York 1981.

[18] Clemence Dane, *Regiment of Women*, Heinemann, London 1966, p.204.

[19] *Ibid*, p.196.

[20] Carol A Senf, 'Dracula: Stoker's Response to the New Woman', *Victorian Studies*, no 26 1982, pp.33-39.

[21] See Christopher Frayling, *The Vampyre*, Gollancz, London 1978.

[22] I do not know of a story of a female werewolf, and the majority of werewolf stories are in part about the notion of the beast that dwells in the breast of the apparently civilised man – in other words, the werewolf image seems to articulate part of our culture's concept of masculinity.

[23] Robin Wood 'An introduction to the American Horror Film' in Bill Nichols (ed), *Movies and Methods II*, University of California Press, Berkeley 1985, pp.195-220.

[24] Bram Stoker, *Dracula*, Penguin 1985, p.52.

[25] Anne Rice, *Interview with the Vampire*, p.248.

[26] Rosemary Jackson, *Fantasy: the Literature of Subversion*, Methuen, London 1981.

[27] Michel Foucault, The History of Sexuality, Pelican 1981.

[28] Jeffrey Weeks, *Sexuality and its Discontents*, Routledge and Kegan Paul, London 1985.

[29] Count Stenbock 'The True Story of a Vampire', *Jeremy* no 2, 1970, pp.20-24.

[30] Sheridan LeFanu, *op cit*, p.387.

[31] Richard Dyer 'Stereotyping', in Dyer (ed), *Gays and Film*, Zoetrope, New York 1984, pp.27-39.

[32] LeFanu *op cit*, p.471.

[33] 'La morte amoureux', (first published in Chronique de Paris, June 23-26, 1836) in Theophile Gautier, *Contes fantastiques*, José Corti, Paris 1962.

[34] *Ibid*, p.118.

[35] Anon, *The Amplified Journal of D.G.*, *Mandate*, July 1986 onwards.

[36] *Dracula*, p.52.

[37] For a brilliant analysis of male passivity, suppressed homoeroticism and the male desire to be penetrated in Dracula, see Christopher Craft 'Kiss me with those Red Lips': Gender and Inversion in Bram Stoker's Dracula', *Representations* no 8, Fall 1984, pp.107-133.

[38] Gautier, *op cit* p.115 (pénétrait is in the original).

[39] *Ibid*, p.112-3.

[40] *I Vampire*, p.178.

[41] Harlan Greene *Why We Never Danced the Charleston*, Penguin 1985, p.26.

[42] Stenbock *op cit*, p.24.

[43] See Alice Walker, *In Search of Our Mothers' Gardens*, The Women's Press, London 1983.

[44] *I Vampire*, p.178.

[45] Second entry *D.G.*, p.60.

[46] *Ibid*, p.88.

[47] *Ibid*, p.71-72.

What is Life Without My Love?: Desire and Romantic Fiction

AMAL TREACHER

What is Life to me without thee?
What is Life to me if thou art dead?
What is Life to me without thee?
What is Life without my Love?[1]

Mills and Boon stories outline, describe, and speak to a certain set of relations and phantasies which permeate our emotions and consciousness. The pull of romantic fiction lies in the way that it engages with certain aspects of the female psyche. In recognition of this, some recent analytic studies of romantic fiction have attempted to shift theoretical criticism of this genre to go beyond its dismissal as escapist junk. For example, Tania Modleski and Ann Barr Snitow from different perspectives have both argued that romantic fiction is a powerful mode of expression for women in that it satiates, albeit briefly, some female needs and desires. This does not mean that feminists should uncritically adopt romantic fiction as a radical intervention into women's lives. But an analysis of romantic fiction offers us clues and insights into the way some women attempt to negotiate the relationship of their phantasy life to their actual life.

Contained within romantic fiction, and articulated with unconscious desires and wishes, are longing, wanting, wishing to possess and to be possessed, erotic phantasies of passivity and activity, the need to be cherished and adored, being both powerful and powerless ... the list is endless.

The problem of outlining these elements is that the unconscious *is unconscious*; it therefore cannot be known in total. It is a slippery, cunning creature. To focus only on desire, wanting and phantasy life, when these elements may merely be the tip of a massive iceberg, could be to miss some vital clues into what constitutes our unconscious lives. This is not to dismiss or devalue the language and theoretical tools available to us, but to argue for caution when we are speaking of/to the unconscious for:

> We may detect the faint shuffle of the slouching beast, and be tempted to throw a set of grappling irons into the darkness, seize him, label him, hang him round with words and haul him prematurely to birth. We may then be stuck with a deformed monster that we may have largely created by our own precipitate verbosity; we may then proceed laboriously onwards with a sort of analytic mistake, while the true creature who is not yet ready for the light of day retreats backwards into the darkness again.[2]

But this is not to argue that our doubts and misgivings should prevent us from grappling with the beast.

There are two broad points of view within feminism about the complex area of female sexuality and its related phantasies. One perspective argues that phantasy can be changed at will. That women have the strength to break their bonds and to shake off the shackles of the patriarchal penis; moreover women should not have demeaning phantasies about power, and penetration; somehow the desire or need, to be protected, ravished and adored, could be made to disappear into a universal black dumping space for all unwanted phantasies, desires and needs.

A second perspective argues that phantasy is intrinsic to human nature, and bound up in some way with sexuality, but that its implications remain to be explored. The dynamics of women's desires and longings are highly complex; and we are a long way from understanding our unconscious and conscious phantasies, and therefore their power, meaning and hold on our psyches. This strand argues that to demand moralistically that women should have the strength to change their lives, feelings, erotic phantasies and needs does not help in the exploration of these feelings. Relying on hope and will does not guarantee the disappearance of these feelings. We cannot radically change ourselves just because we wholeheartedly wish to do so. Part of the project within this perspective of feminist writings is to discover why we are as we are: social gendered beings, with a whole range of contradictory and ambivalent feelings, known and unknown thoughts, and conscious and unconscious phantasies. Thus there is a need to explore women's actual sexual longings in order to understand how power and desire are inextricably interlinked. As Lynne Segal has pointed out, power is knotted through with desire and pleasure in ways which may either support or amend the general relations of dominance and submission which exist between men and women.[3] This perspective also attempts to analyse how aspects of our psyches and collective social histories permeate, and reverberate through, our longings, and emotional and sexual relations.

This article is firmly located within the latter perspective of feminism, and draws upon psychoanalytic work to edge towards an exploration of some female sexual longings and wishes, in order to try to understand how seemingly undesirable phantasies remain obstinately erotic.

There are probably few things that have obsessed men and women as much as love. The questions range from the abstract if despairing enquiry, 'what is love?', to the depressed and anxious scream, 'am I loved/loveable, will anybody be able to love me enough?', or 'can I love another, love someone else enough?'. The longing for love, nagging doubts, and intellectual and emotional questions pervade us all, and touch us all at what appears to be the centre of our being. To explore our longings, sexual desires and needs, together with the concept of love itself, is difficult and painful because it brings into question so much of what we experience as our very self. But love and sexual desire are not pure, ahistoric, asocial and untainted forces; they are shot through with a variety of emotional needs and wishes: to obtain approval, lessen anxiety, to be able to depend upon another, and to repair pyschic hurts that have arisen from the experiences of being rejected, disappointed and humiliated.[4] It is to this love-absorbed core of self that romantic fiction appeals: romantic fiction positively worships and is totally preoccupied with love.

In *Say Hello to Yesterday*,[5] Holly Weston, the central female protagonist, is a photo-journalist who is sent to a Greek island by her paper. While there she meets Nick Falconer, the husband from whom she has been separated for the last seven years. The narrative unfolds with Holly remembering her brief marriage to Nick. They had met when she was sixteen and he twenty-two, and fallen passionately in love. Against strong parental objections they had married. But wedded bliss was soon to end. Nick had been made to feel inferior and ashamed because of his background and Holly's parents, especially her mother, had let him know that he was not one of them, lacking in social graces and awkward in his endeavours to please. After six months things came to a head and Nick left. By this time Holly had become pregnant, unknown to Nick. After being pressurised to terminate the pregnancy and to get a divorce, Holly had finally broken with her parents, belatedly realising that they were responsible for the break-up of her relationship. When the story begins her son Jaimie is six years old and she has a new career as a photo-journalist, a cottage in the country and a housekeeper. Holly is courted by Felix Riddell, the man she has come to interview. She turns him down partly because he tried too hard to make himself attractive to her, unlike Nick who 'never had to put on an act to make himself attractive … he possessed an arrant masculinity that made women physically aware and drew them to him like a magnet'.[6] However, Nick is jealous of the time Holly spends with Felix – 'Even through the thickness of the towel, she could feel his grip on her shoulders. "Have you been to bed with him yet? Have you", he demanded savagely'.[7] In turn Holly is convinced that Nick is having an affair with a sophisticated French woman who has been making non-too-subtle advances towards Nick.

The narrative is full of passionate arguments/
encounters:

> He reached out to grab her, but she was in such a blind fury,
> beating against his chest with her fists, trying to claw at his
> face, that it took a few minutes for him to catch her wrists and
> twist them behind her back. Even then Holly still struggled
> and fought; twisting in his arms and arching her body as she
> sought vainly to get free.[8]

There are also many misunderstandings, and denied and
acknowledged attraction:

> ... when he helped her off the boat and held her in his arms
> she had wanted him to kiss her, wanted urgently to feel his
> mouth on hers, to have his hands touch her until he had
> roused her to the peak of desire ...[9]

Finally Nick and Holly (with a sigh of frustrated relief
from this reader) make love.

Love Would Be Easy If You
Were The Colour Of My Dreams

The narrative focuses on, and leads the reader to, the
crucial declaration of love between the lovers; it is at the
point, when the man reveals 'I love you', and, 'I've never
stopped loving you, and I'm never going to let you go
again', that the story finishes. For the reader the
inevitability of the discovery of love between the two
characters does not hinder the anticipation, the excitement and the longing for that moment. It is precisely
within and through that certain safe knowledge that the
anticipated pleasure can be increased, and this security is
intertwined with the pleasure gained 'in returning again
and again to that breathless, ambivalent nervous state
before certainty or satiety'.[10]

Within this genre love is represented as a powerful and
consuming force which stands over and above the lovers, a

power in the face of which they have no control and even less responsibility. The painful knowledge about the difficulties involved in love and relationships is kept firmly outside the narrative, thereby enabling the reader while reading, to believe that the only task involved in relationships is that of proper truthful communication and understanding. In *Say Hello to Yesterday* the true reunion between Nick and Holly only occurs when Holly discovers the extent of her parents involvement in destroying her marriage to Nick. It is in the last chapter that the reader, and Holly, discovers that Nick had not abandoned her, but had desperately tried to contact Holly only to be lied to by her parents. It is Holly's parents, not Nick, who betray her. Believing in this implausible scenario is a pleasurable suspension of everyday experience, made possible since fiction is in some ways a closed system that by-passes much of what we know and believe about relationships and our actual world of experience. As Ann Barr Snitow has argued, the ability of the language of fiction to by-pass our existing knowledges constitutes part of our pleasure in reading.[11] Romantic fiction does not ask why our relationships fail, why we struggle and get disappointed, for this genre is firmly based on the belief that love and the lovers are blameless. It is at the point where most relationships encounter difficulties and the mundane that the narrative stops: not for Mills and Boon lovers the arguments over the wedding arrangements, the boredom over the breakfast boiled egg, or the drudgery of domesticity. It is at the point where it would be difficult, if not downright impossible, to sustain the sexual aura and rather frantic emotionality that the story stops. It has no more to say.

Romantic fiction speaks to, and satiates, conscious and unconscious needs for love and relationships to be simple, clear and yet passionate. However, the genre resonates with the unconscious wish for love to cure and heal past hurts, and the regressive desire to be unconditionally loved. These unconscious and primitive needs are formed through and within our infantile experiences of parenting, of feeling inadequately loved, unnurtured and abandoned. No infant is unconditionally loved, and this can stand in direct contradiction to the desire for, and phantasy of total adoration. The impossibility of these demands does not necessarily diminish the phantasies, and our involvement with our mothers and fathers is a blueprint for our adult sexual and emotional relationships

In *Female Sexuality* (1931) Freud persuasively argued that the little girl's enduring and intense attachment is to her primary love object: the mother. This devoted bond of the daughter to the mother is the original relationship and all subsequent relationships are built on that tie ... 'the main content of her development to womanhood lay in the carrying over of her affective object attachments from her mother to her father'.[12] This carrying over of attachments from the mother to the father is fundamentally interlinked with the shift of sexual activity from the clitoris (the active) to the vagina (the passive). For the little boy his Oedipal passage is simpler, his site of sexual activity (the penis), and his primary love object (the mother), remain the same. For the boy his primary and continuing love object is heterosexual, and for the little girl her primary love object is homosexual, and then heterosexual; bisexuality is therefore a strong disposition in all women. The passage through the Oedipus complex is painful and difficult for all, but it is a crucial event as it is the means by which each individual finds his/her place in the social and cultural community.

Most analyses of Mills and Boon argue that the books are shot through with 'phallic worship' and that the male protagonist is firmly in the role of the patriarch, the phallus, the omnipotent ideal father

> who only wants the heroine (favourite daughter) ... his desire for her is so strong, so overwhelming that she can only respond. All obstacles which exist for this kind of love are cleared away; they are only the result of misunderstandings. In the end the father is restored to his 'original position'. He has total control but he is basically kind and will provide for her.[13]

In *Say Hello to Yesterday* Nick is the virile, dominant,

attractive male: the all powerful patriarch. But he does not just dominate, thrust and possess, he also protects, cherishes, nurtures and adores. The hero is endowed with maternal qualities; he is not simply the phallus but also the maternal phallus: the ideal mother and father. This fundamental desire of daughters – that they should be what their father loves above all else[14] – is transferred over to the lover. Daughters want to be the most desired object of their mothers and fathers. The parents are absent from the Mills and Boon narrative, denied and killed off, because they have disappointed, they are superfluous; it is now the hero who will always gratify, who will be in loco parentis. The woman, Holly, has the man, Nick, who is both mother and father. Holly is able to move 'into the safe haven of his (Nick's/father's/mother's) arms' and her 'happiness is complete and overflowing because she has arrived home'.[15]

Freud argues that the child's phantasy life is imbued with real recollections from a time when the parents were exalted by the child. The power of Mills and Boon romances is that in portraying the hero as the ideal mother and father they return the reader to the longing for what Freud described as 'the happy vanished days when his (her) father seemed to him (her) the noblest and strongest of men and his (her) mother the dearest and loveliest of women'.[16] Mills and Boon reverberate to the unconscious phantasies, which do not disappear even in adult life, of the ideal combined parent believed in in earlier years. The wish for the total love of the mother and father becomes the longing for that total love to be located within one's partner in adult life.

It is as if through possessing and identifying with this ideal love, one can become the ideal person: for women, the phallic daughter and therefore also the phallic mother. Laplanche and Pontalis define the phallic mother as a

woman endowed, in phantasy, with a phallus. This image has two main forms: the woman is represented either as having an external phallus or phallic attribute, or else as having preserved the male's phallus inside herself.[17]

Freud argued that it was at the moment when the little girl recognises that she has been castrated that the Oedipal complex is initiated. It is the knowledge of her lack that wounds the little girl's narcissistic sense of self. The little girl still desires a penis and then a child by her father which is merely a substitute for the penis itself. Phantasy therefore fills the void, the absent centre for the little girl, and leads, I would suggest, to the wish to identify with the male hero, the patriarch, as a route into the phantasised possession of the penis. Further, the penis is 'incorporated' through intercourse. Through these unconscious routes of identification and incorporation the girl/woman repairs her own damaged narcissistic sense of self, and her mother's disappointment and ambivalence about having produced a daughter. The woman becomes empowered through being able to possess the phallus, thereby gaining phallic attributes, and also by being able to preserve the phallus 'inside herself'.

The most powerful figure in *Say Hello To Yesterday* is Holly's mother who is nameless. Whilst both parents are accused of having blocked love's true path, it is really Holly's mother who is blamed. She is represented as cruel, snobbish and, in her constant denigration of Nick, castrating. She is the powerful figure: the phallic mother. It is only when Holly discovers that she is pregnant – and has therefore received and retained the paternal phallus – that she can leave her parents. It is through Jamie, her son, the 'centre of her existence', that she finds some financial and emotional independence.

Love is imbued with many unconscious desires and needs, but one strong dynamic wish is for Love to be a magic force which will cure and heal all rifts, wounds and past hurts. Romantic fiction is shot through with the belief 'that it is possible really to be taken care of and to achieve that state of self-transcendence and self-forgetfulness promised by the ideology of love'.[18] Perhaps reading romantic fiction can itself partly fulfil these desires. We do not just desire that love will transform us and our lives; that wish is drenched with our need to be loved unconditionally because of the very fact of our existence.

The need for love in childhood is boundless: 'it demands exclusive possession, it is not content with less than all'.[19] And this is true of the romantic fiction heroines who 'are loved as babies are loved, simply because they exist'.[20]

In *Say Hello to Yesterday* love is represented as unconditional. Nick is able to avow his love for Holly, and therefore heal their past rifts and difficulties:

> He made love to her again then, rediscovering a long-forgotten fire that had blazed and burned so long ago. It was different and yet the same as she remembered. Love and gentleness were there now, as well as heat and passion. Bitterness disappeared as they gloried in each other's sensuality, lifted to dizzying heights of ecstasy that washed away all hurts and fears.[21]

Whilst reading, the stories satiate and satisfy the need for unconditional love, and further confirm the phantasy that it can be, will be, and is, possible to be unconditionally and totally loved.

The act of reading, by its very nature, is a private and absorbing activity, which requires that others are pushed out, while one enters a space where the shutters are down and a dream is spun. By reading the romantic story the desire to love oneself is satisfied by identifying with the lovers – *both* hero and heroine. I can only write about this process in the personal. My identification is often with *both* characters, sometimes simultaneously, more often it shifts from one to the other with little apparent rhyme or reason. But whichever, I am utterly involved in the story. It captures the whole of my interest. I pick up and read romantic fiction when I am feeling depressed, unloved and unloveable, and somehow, through the process of reading, I manage to feel loved even if in fleeting and intangible moments. What the books satiate, even if very fleetingly, is the longing to be loved to feel full, whole, integrated, and to be both powerful and powerless in the face of love and sexual desire. Love would be easy, if you, I and love itself, were the colour of my dreams.

Wings of Desire

Romantic fiction is permeated with contradictory phantasies of being powerful and yet powerless, of possessing and not possessing, of having total control and no control whatsoever, of being passive and simultaneously active. Sex is romanticised and love depicted as a pure emotion. The two forces are conflated and often represented as if love can be substituted for sex, and sex for love. The narrative is positively shot through with sexual energy, tension and action. Ann Barr Snitow argues that love is a code word for fuck: love is but a metaphor. Drawing upon the work of Peter Parisi, she asserts that romantic novels are essentially pornographic and that sex is the real reason for the existence of these novels. They offer a specific sexual release for those who believe that sex without love is wrong. The romance and the promised marriage exist as salves to the conscience.[22]

Romantic fiction quite clearly expresses the need to be found desirable, wantable and sexually attractive by the male/father. Holly obviously wants Nick to love her, and to be sexually attracted to her; Nick 'possessed this arrant masculinity' and was 'a tall, handsome man, with a strong and beautifully proportioned body; a man with a dominant masculinity that would physically attract any woman'.[23] Holly had 'been so proud, so over the moon with joy when, of all the girls who had wanted him, he had chosen her', and he had 'told her that he was a one woman man, and then had taken her in his arms and convinced her that she was definitely that one woman'.[24] The complex wishes to possess another, to be possessed and to be utterly possessed in the face of an overwhelming emotion are naturalised within the narrative, and partly satiated by identification with the heroine. Any fear or anxiety about being taken over by another is dispelled, all that remains is the excitement:

turning, she plunged into the sea and began to swim, her mind filled with the way he had said *my wife*. He had meant it only as a snub for the other woman, she knew, but it made her remember the way he used to say it when they were first married, with such pride and possessiveness, *as if she was the most precious thing in his life* ... Nick stepped forward and put a hand on her shoulder in the *age old possessive gesture of a male for his mate*.[25] (my italics)

Romantic fiction does represent the sexuality of woman as partly passive. The woman is seen as not able, nor having the right, to actively and consciously pursue and seduce the man. Female sexuality is partly represented as a force for male pleasure: the heroine is constantly in a state of half-aroused sexual desire for the hero: her movements and actions are for him alone. Throughout the narrative the woman is sexualised and is represented in such a manner that the reader views her through 'sensual coloured glasses'. On the beach Holly is described thus:

> she reached up to clip her hair up at the back, her body tall and slender in a dusty pink bikini, her legs long and shapely ... the water wrapped around her like a warm blanket, unbelievably soft and caressing[26]

The woman is presented as ready for, and passively awaiting, her next sexual encounter, the next sensual charge with the man. The hero (when described in sexual terms) is hard, thrusting, with animal masculinity, a ruthless sexuality, domineering, assured and possessing inborn command and authority. The heroine is ready and waiting for this icon of perfect sexual masculinity.

However, in private, the heroine's thoughts are actually highly erotic, active and full of more or less explicit hints as to her wishes ...

> she had lain awake, thinking about him, her body still hot and frustrated from the way he had kissed her, caressed her. The thought of his fingers touching her made her toss and turn on the bed, longing for fulfilment. She wanted him to take her, she knew that, wanted it desperately, after those long empty years.[27]

It is on her own, in her wandering erotic daydreams and thoughts that the woman can be active and powerful, and can express what she wants in terms of sex, and her male lover.

The anxiety for many women is that they will be nothing without the man and therefore the penis: an empty vessel waiting to be filled in a state of throbbing frustration. These romantic fiction phantasies, and many female sexual phantasies, are contradictory. They contain the desire

> to be blindly ravished, to melt, and the desire to be spiritually adored, saved from the humiliation of dependence and sexual passivity through the agency of a protective male who will somehow make reparation to the woman he loves for her powerlessness[28]

The narrative constructs the hero as this icon of sexuality, but he is also romanticised, and along with the heroine placed at the centre of the tale. He is what we women want. We read on as the woman gets this romantic sexual prize. Woman are reduced to a longing: a longing for the penis/phallus, the man, and if these desired objects are not possessed and gained, the woman is empty, unnatural and powerless: 'with a groan, he thrust himself deep inside her, filling the throbbing emptiness so completely ...' ... 'he filled the aching void so completely'.[29] It is not just the love, but also the penis, of a good man which can now heal and fill up the aching void.

'Holly ran her fingers over his chest, touching, exploring, rediscovering her power over him'.[30] Female sexuality is represented as powerful and woman as all-powerful in her sexuality and femininity. This power remains within the realm of sexuality and femininity, but this is hardly surprising since most representations of female sexuality alternate between woman as passive and as all-powerful. These polarised representations of female sexuality symbolise commonly felt sexual frissons:

> the titillation has little to do with any physical event. It is a 'social drama' and exists in the anticipation, anxiety, suspense

and fear of waiting for the manifestation of – the impossible.
The impossible longing is to be both helpless and in control,
ravished and adored, powerless and yet supremely
powerful.[31]

Except for in the last sexual encounter, Holly always
withdraws from the scene leaving Nick in a state of
emotional turmoil. Holly is the pivot of the narrative in
that it is she who decides when sexual intercourse takes
place. She thereby has total control over the timing of the
climax of the relationship.

The male's often impossible sexual bullying is to some
extent excused by the narrative – his behaviour is
represented as being caused by his overwhelming love and
desire. Many analysts of romantic fiction have interpreted
this aspect of the genre as a way of side-stepping the
difficulties in uneven power gender relationships –
women can reassure themselves that their men behave
badly only because of their overpowering love. However,
romantic fiction illustrates that male sexuality too is
contradictory, involving complex desires for dependency,
submission and forgiveness. Men envy and fear women as
well as wanting to dominate and control them. These
stories play on our knowledge of male and female
contradictory sexual feelings. They make points of
difference between men and women exciting. They allow
for, and satiate, the dynamics of sexual tension and
frisson.

Grappling With The Beast

Elizabeth Cowie, in her essay 'Fantasia', argues that one of
the important elements of phantasy is that it does not fix:
through and within phantasy characters and scenarios
shift, are in a state of flux and ambiguity. Phantasies are
both the expression of a wish, and the fulfilment of a wish.
They are linked into unconscious desires and unconscious
scenes; they are also elaborations of these. A dream is
re-worked in order to place some order and coherence
onto the material which has been created by the

unconscious mechanisms of displacement and conden-
sation. The re-working draws upon the dream, the
subject's day-dreams, and the scenarios already in
existence to create a narrative of coherence and
continuity.[32] Similarly, romantic fiction narratives give
some order and coherence to the wild, contradictory and
ambivalent unconscious and its phantasies. But this
coherence is fluid, it is not fixed. The characters are
shallow and empty. And this is precisely the narrative's
forte rather than its failing. The shallowness allows the
characters and the scenarios to be filled up with the
reader's own unconscious. Imagination is at play
fluctuating between identifying with the passive and the
active: the penetrator and the penetrated.

This ability of phantasy to unfix that which is seemingly
stable means that power cannot be simply located within
the hero/phallus. Much of the narrative is centred on the
hero's own longing for the heroine's love. In *Say Hello To
Yesterday* it is Nick who pursues Holly – literally around the
world. He is almost brought to his knees before he can
possess her. It is this aspect of romantic fiction which is its
attraction for Tania Modleski: 'a great deal of our
satisfaction in reading these novels comes, I am convinced,
from the elements of a revenge fantasy, from our
conviction that the woman is bringing the man to his knees
and that while he is being so hateful, he is internally
grovelling, grovelling, grovelling ...'.[33]

The hero becomes aware of how precious the heroine is
after she has run away. This childish phantasy that only
after we have disappeared will our true value be
appreciated conceals a deep-seated desire for vengeance.
It is only once Nick has proved his utter devotion to Holly
that he is rewarded with the gift of his son. It is at that
point that Holly can move into 'the safe haven of his arms'.
It is up to the hero to repair and make good the heroine's
loss, and lack of power, and yet neither the heroine nor
the reader are submissive or passive in this act of
reparation.

Love, the penis/phallus, is permeated with the unconscious desire to heal, make whole and allow for feelings of

fulfilment. As Freud has convincingly argued, the effects of our first identifications and relationships with others will permeate and reverberate throughout the rest of our lives. The shift from the mother to the father, for women, is neither smooth nor ever complete. The traces and effects of that first profound love are omnipresent. Phantasies which occur from our first emotional relationships remain and influence our adult lives. These phantasies play an important part in the romantic fiction narrative. Romantic fiction speaks to, and resonates with, these phantasies.

Romantic fiction can make the world seem like a warm, better, more loveable place and indeed the more difficult our lives, the more depressing the social world becomes, the more likely we are to turn to phantasies of glamour, wealth, happiness and love in order to seek a necessary distraction from the increasingly depressing world in which we exist. But this is not to dismiss or patronise romantic fiction, but to argue that one of its functions is to reassure us that the world is peopled with men and women who are certain of what and who they are, in gender and sexuality. Ambivalence, contradictions and doubts are left outside of the narrative. Disappointment in our lovers, or in our sexual and emotional relationships, is swept aside. Romantic fiction actively resists the social, or any mention of obligation and duty. It revels in the primitive, the emotional, the regressive. The difficulty remains that

> what is wrong with our lives is perhaps not so much the lack of orgasms [emotional highs, A.T.] as our perpetual craving for that orgasm [emotional high] which can obliterate the isolation and emptiness we feel in the rest of our lives.[34]

And as most of us struggle daily against suffering, feeling alone/lonely, and juggle about our duties and responsibilities, who can truthfully resist the offer of an escape through the possibility of hearing this promise:

> Dunc's eyes were liquid with desire. I want your sweetness, your comfort, your strength. I want your love. I want to be surrounded by it, to lose myself in it. And if you'll give me that Anne I'll give my life'.[35]

Many thanks to Sally Alexander, Claudia Lank and Susannah Radstone for their help, criticism and support.

Notes

[1] 'What is life to me without thee?' aria from Gluck's Orfeo, made popular in the 1940s by Kathleen Ferrier.

[2] Nina Coltart, 'Slouching towards Bethlehem' in Gregorio Kohon (ed), *The British School of Psychoanalysis: The Independent Tradition*, Free Association Books 1986, p.190.

[3] Lynne Segal, 'Sensual Uncertainty, or Why the Clitoris is not Enough' in Sue Cartledge and Joanna Ryan (eds), *Sex and Love*, The Women's Press 1983, p.41.

[4] *Ibid*, p.44.

[5] Sally Wentworth, *Say Hello to Yesterday*, Mills and Boon 1984.

[6] *Ibid*, p.148.

[7] *Ibid*, p.159.

[8] *Ibid*, p.103.

[9] *Ibid*, p.112.

[10] Ann Barr Snitow, 'Mass Market Romance: Pornography for Women is Different' in Snitow, Stansell and Thompson (eds), *Desire: The Politics of Sexuality*, Virago Press 1984, p.263.

[11] *Ibid*, p.264.

[12] Sigmund Freud, 'Female Sexuality' in *On Sexuality*, Pelican Freud Library, No 7, 1977.

[13] Rosalind Coward, *Female Desire: Women's Sexuality Today*, Paladin, 1984, p.195.

[14] Freud, *op cit*.

[15] Wentworth, *op cit*, p.188.

[16] Sigmund Freud, 'Family Romances', in *On Sexuality*, Pelican 1977, p.225.

[17] J Laplanche and J B Pontalis, *The Language of Psychoanalysis*, Hogarth Press 1985, p.311.

[18] Tania Modleski, *Loving with a Vengeance*, Methuen 1984, p.37.

[19] Sigmund Freud, 'Female Sexuality', *op cit*, p.378.

[20] Barr Snitow, *op cit*, p.269.

[21] Wentworth, *op cit*, p.181.

[22] Barr Snitow, *op cit*, p.267.

[23] Wentworth, *op cit*, p.44.

[24] *Ibid*, p.44.

[25] *Ibid*, p.99.

[26] *Ibid*, p.36

[27] *Ibid*, p.136.

[28] Segal, *op cit*, p.46.

[29] Jane Silverwood, *Voyage of the Heart*, Mills and Boon 1985, p.103.

[30] Wentworth, *op cit*, p.174.

[31] Segal, *op cit*, p.41.
[32] Elizabeth Cowie, 'Fantasia', in *MF* No 9, 1984.
[33] Modleski, *op cit*, p.45.
[34] Segal, *op cit*, p.46.
[35] Silverwood, *op cit*, p.220.

The Inverstigators: Lesbian Crime Fiction

SALLY MUNT

The classic detective story ends in a library, with a moment of revelation. Likewise, all my clues are gathered, and my textual witnesses are bound and expectant in front of me. And so I am entrusted to give you the definitive explanation, I become the purveyor of meaning. Then I can return to my marrows or my knitting.

But I cannot give you me, reading, until I have told you of another ending: my mother's death. Her funeral was six months ago yesterday, and I am retelling myself around it. So, I am reading lesbian crime fiction and grieving. This is important.

I want to tell you about cancer, but I can't. I saw my mother shrivel, over five months, from a 66 year old woman who went rollerskating and trampolining, to a corpse. I would lift her on and off the toilet, and in the bath, sponge up the pools of water collecting in the hollow which was her chest. The huge tumours in her stomach and liver were her only bulk, and she would pat them, and wonder at them, like one does a child. The last days and nights in the hospice were spent holding her hand, holding on to her for both of us, my breathing in rhythm with her rattle. I felt I was dying with her; she went in (our) sleep.

Waiting, I was in continual suspension, a state of dread. For five months every time the phone rang I thought 'this is it'; I still flinch. The cancer was the mystery – we didn't understand it, only its shadow, a negative, a growing silhouette. This inevitable death had a murderer of sorts, but one with no motive. I had a body but no explanation. So, I read books full of bodies and reasons: crime novels, dozens of them.

In retrospect I make my own narratives (over and over) of my mother's dying. I want my anxiety assuaged. I want to make meaning and cohesion out of this loss. I want to see it in my palm and know it, and close my hand, into a fist. I tell my friends that I am fine, except for a touch of back-ache, cystitis, flu or tiredness. And I read a lot.

First there were novels of self-discovery and romance, personal narratives of development, and then a couple of years ago it was science fiction, and utopian vision. Now when I walk into a women's bookshop I see crime novels, often by authors I consider anti-feminist; it's disconcerting. Friends who used to read Alice Walker now ask me if I've read the new P D James. A new type of fiction is appearing, lesbian crime, in which sexy superdykes stride the city streets in their steel-capped DMs, swinging their double-headed axe, slayed patriarchs in their wake. Or so you'd imagine. Almost all the novels present the figure of a woman on the cover, foregrounding the lone hera[1] against a darkened building, a synecdochal city.

> When we see a tall dark man walking down a damp, shadowy street wearing a snap-brim hat, trench coat, and gun and hear the melancholy note of the blues trumpet wail up and over the sound of his footsteps on the pavement, we know everything we need to know about him. He is the man who goes unafraid down mean streets, the man who is the best in his world and yet is good enough for any world: the detective hero.[2]

Robert Skinner's cameo encapsulates the essence of the hard-boiled dick. The low-lit, monochromatic American *film noir* of the 1940s springs to mind, with its city of mysteries and shadows, violence and vengeance. Through the mist steps the 'man in the mac', dispenser of commonsense justice, alone in his mission. The image is archetypal – the warrior knight, the tough cowboy, the intrepid explorer – he is the representative of Man, and yet more than a man, he is the focus of morality, the controlled centre surrounded by chaos, the Hero. An effective reading prescribes identification with this mediator of all action, meaning, and pleasure.

Can this historically monological mysogynistic megalomaniac be transformed by a lesbian-feminist reading? Two archetypal traits lend the potential.

Firstly, he is a crusader, traditionally representing and re-asserting with moral certitude the status quo, a redemptive figure, single-handedly stemming the tide of chaos; his morality of unequivocal self-assertion reflects the cult of individualism recently revitalised by Thatcherism. Some aspects of feminism are also characterised by tendencies of evangelism; this is often tempered, in the later 1980s, by a (post-feminist?) re-emphasis on 'self'. It seems to me that the communality and political activism of the 1970s and early 1980s is being supplanted by an individualistic inertia, a retraction in the face of hegemonic hostility.

Secondly, the detective hero is an outlaw, and here the parallel with lesbianism is clear. He is alone, isolated, on the edge, an observer, not a participator. This motif of lesbian identity has been imposed and internalised ever since *The Well of Loneliness*, occasionally transformed by an inversion which endows lesbians with a superior vantage point from which to analyse the vagaries of institutionalised heterosexuality.

The detective hero exhibits a paradox: he is at once a representative of society and a critique of it. Lesbian-feminist crime novels tend to produce a particular version of this antithesis. Manifestly they are opposed to patriarchy; implicitly however they depend on many aspects of the mainstream genre, such as an overriding Manichean morality of good versus evil, notions of unified subjectivity, innateness, natural justice, and tidy textual closures. These can be addressed as masculine forms. In this essay I plan to look closely at several of these novels in order to discern whether, and if so how, they subvert or are constrained by the genre of the traditional crime novel. As far as they do conform to this historic type, I propose that this potentially inhibits a radical reading. These novels, however, have evolved primarily out of lesbian, not crime, fiction. This literary practice has inevitably been preoccupied with issues of sexuality and identity. For many women it serves as a way of rendering explicit their re/suppressed desire. Thus I would like to explore how subversive, given their conflated (and conflictual?) generic positioning, these texts can be.

To this end I have employed a Foucauldian perspective assuming that resistance to sexual conventions is significantly constrained by the character of discourse itself.[3] I try to indicate how – because that space has already been defined for us – articulating our own meanings is, to borrow Annette Kolodny's term, a minefield.[4] To illustrate: do the novels, by simply substituting the strong hero with the strong hera, push the reader into a limiting 'identity politics' reminiscent of the images of women protagonists of the 1970s?[5] Do these texts, in short, undermine themselves by attacking reductionism and then employing it as a form of resistance? (Replacing 'all lesbians are bad' with 'all lesbians are good', for example.)

Amateur City by Katherine V Forrest introduces Kate Delafield, of the Los Angeles Police Department.[6] Both *Amateur City* and its sequel *Murder at the Nightwood Bar*[7] are unusual in presenting a lesbian cop, a focus, perhaps, for forbidden fantasies. Kate is the archetypal soft-centred butch, as a cop 'one of the best' (p.90), a Vietnam vet, who quit law school at the prospect of defending a 'possible criminal' (p.62). Her 'strong face, those grim features' (p.33) are 'tight polished planes' (p.113), her cold blues eyes impersonal and impervious to tears. Her body is 'firmly muscled … solid … flatter, tighter' showing 'steeliness' and 'unmistakable strength' (p.115). Her hatchet features, tempered by tragedy – the death of her parents and the incineration of her lover in a car crash – are at times a 'waxen mask of suffering' (p.110). This tragic hera has an Othelloan flaw:

> The tired knowledge that always she was silhouetted against her background.
> Always.
> Always. Growing up she had been taller and stronger, more aggressive than the other girls; in look and manner, hopelessly unfeminine by their standards. Among similarly uniformed women in the Marine Corps, she had been resented for her unusual physical strengths and command presence. She had been the woman reluctantly singled out ...
> And always there had been that one most essential difference: she was a woman who desired only other women. (p.24)

Terms inferring states of sexual darkness, 'essential difference', are reminiscent of Radclyffe Hall: 'a narrative of damnation, of the lesbian's suffering as a lonely outcast'.[8] Havelock Ellis'[9] refined definition of 'congenital invert' relies on the visible presence of male physical attributes, and Kate Delafield's appearance is paradigmatically masculinised.

Historically women have been drawn to the police and military as professions promising vocational strength and control, and this alliance with the state also upholds the vision of social integration, the need to belong exacerbated by the very difference which excludes. Kate was born in 1946 and her cultural backdrop is lesbian rather than lesbian-feminist: 'All my upbringing, my influences were from the fifties' (p.120); and her ground-level politics are informed by that period of reactionary repression.

However, Kate's ambivalent position does liberate an objectivity often highly critical of the Los Angeles Police Department's grosser prejudices. Her sidekick, Detective Ed Taylor, embodies a morality we suppose typical of a redneck dick, and Kate's longsuffering disgust highlights both her incongruity and his unquestioned bigotry. In *Murder at the Nightwood Bar* the structures of alienation are reversed, for the Nightwood Bar is a lesbian bar, and Taylor's intimidatory tactics are derided, his masculinity a magnet to ridicule. This is Kate's territory:

> She felt stripped of her grey gabardine pants and jacket, her
> conservative cloak of invisibility in the conventional world. In
> here she was fully exposed against her natural background.
> She recognised aspects of herself in each of the women
> staring back at her ...(p.11)

Although lesbianism is described in terms of disclosing a
natural centre, this image does suggest a more radical
notion of subjectivity. Kate begins to see her identity not in
terms of being a single coherent individual but a
'self-in-relation', in the reflection and diffraction of the
other women's eyes. This progresses away from the liberal
humanist assumption of personal coherence and agency,
the ideology of autonomy which strives to disguise the way
discourses impose themselves and construct us. Identity,
then, consists of a collection of inconsistent and even
contradictory subject positions which compete for allegiance. To recognise oneself as being split is not to wallow
in self-pitying pieces; rather, this displacement of selves
across a range of diverse discourses is implicitly dialectical:
'... in the fact that the subject is a *process* lies the possibility
of transformation'.[10] During the progression of the
narrative Kate increasingly interfuses with the life of the
bar, a movement of inclusion and self-revelation. In the
final few pages she relinquishes her role as romantic
outsider and attends Los Angeles Gay Pride Parade.
Through symbolic tears she sees the thousands of lesbians
and gays who embody a new (for her) *communitas*. The
moment of closure and resolution in *Murder at the
Nightwood Bar* is not the arrest of the murderer but the
integration of one lonely dyke into her culture.

The novel attempts to tackle a tapestry of issues weaving
in and out of the designation *sexual politics*. The victim,
Dory Quillin, is an angel/devil, virgin/whore, child/woman
enigma who has been subjected to sexual abuse by her
father from the age of five. This is an issue dear to the
hearts of lesbians and gay men, so often identified with
child molesters in the paradigm 'deviance'. The Quillins,
Flora and Ronald, represent archetypal American
respectability; the inference is clear. Flora Quillin is

trapped by deceit and denial, a victim of both her husband and religious fundamentalism: the principle of male authority. The destruction at the centre of the biological family is held in opposition to Dory's 'real family, her own people' (p.175); the bartender Maggie spells out to Taylor the number of gays and lesbians rejected by their parents and siblings, asserting '… we have the power in us to make our own families' (p.174). The notion of family is central to the text; there is room for diversity in the lesbian family, an alliance formed by necessity for comfort and political expediency. But can this alternative model offer only a defensive refuge? The final image of the biological family is a poignant plea for inclusion. On the parade Kate sees a banner:

> PARENTS AND FRIENDS OF LESBIANS AND GAYS.
> She stood, applauding with all the others, as the large contingent walked by holding their placards. Her eyes fastened on a man and woman … each with their arms around a young blonde girl between them; and she saw the sign the entwined hands of the parents were holding aloft:
> WE LOVE OUR GAY DAUGHTER. (p.180)

A common humanity which includes homosexuals does not, however extend to criminals; thus the organising structure us/them is not significantly changed, merely the criteria of membership:

> 'I think it's worth trying to take from the streets creatures who don't deserve to live among human beings.' (p.92)

Kate's theory about uncleared homicides generally being committed by 'anonymous roving monsters', together with references to 'subhumans', and Quillin's 'scummy worthless life' combine to categorise 'deviance':

> Even under ideal conditions, she thought venomously, his crime would not qualify him for the electric chair. Not in California where the prerequisite for the death penalty was murder of a particularly heinous nature, the always

problematic 'special circumstances'. Wishing such pun-
ishment on Roland Quillin was irrational and vindictive, she
conceded; monster that he was, the death penalty seemed like
a basic waste of creatures like him. They should instead suffer
the more useful fate of assignment for scientific study and
experiment, for whatever could be gleaned from a malign
cannibal subspecies which had lost the moral right to be
treated as anything other than laboratory fodder. (p.151)

This model of innate depravity derives from a primitive
religious dualism, good/evil. Thus the sex-offender is not
sick, but sinful.[11] This allows no notion of culturally and
historically constructed subjectivity, but depends on a
perception of human conscience as universal and
inherent.[12] If Man is depicted as a rational agent imbued
with an ethical code who is free to transgress, then by
choosing to do so he cannot cease to be human. The text
constructs crime as being against nature, and the offender
as unnatural. Criminals become commonsensically 'other';
labelling deviants as non-human in this way exonerates
society.

The terms of biological determinism extend to an
analysis of lesbianism; Taylor runs the gamut of its causes,
social and psychological, and finally Kate explains to Flora
Quillin why Dory would 'do such a thing':

... I think your daughter loved other women because it was
her nature. A lot of people are just simply that way ... (p.170)

This essentialist definition of homosexuality as an
inherent, and immutable state is, lamentably, often used
by the Gay Liberation movement to establish homosexuals
as member citizens of the liberal pluralist society which
rejects homosexuality when perceived as a political – and
therefore subversive – act.

I have a real problem with these two books; politically I
diverge pretty strongly away from the worldview they
represent. But I loved them. But there again, I also think
Sergeant Lucy Bates of *Hill Street Blues*, Ms Davenport,
and even Captain Frank Furillo are wonderful. I think

some of the many pleasures are: firstly, the fantasies of power, control, and definition/naming that being a law-enforcer permits; secondly, revenge – patriarchs get gruesomely murdered; thirdly, the enigma is resolved and it is always comforting to feel that in that restoration of order the good end happily, the bad unhappily. In fact the mechanisms are different but the pleasure is the same: threat is expunged by the action of the protagonist. Thus my (mythical) security is restored.

The function of the generic convention of the crime novel is the assurance of cohesion, and the containment of threat and danger. This presupposes a level of readerly angst/fear/suspense – call it what you will. In her analysis of gothic novels,[13] Tania Modleski proposes that they provide a release for women's feelings of estrangement, disorientation, and importantly *paranoia*. One suspected cause of paranoia is social isolation, and if this is a problem for heterosexual women, how much more so for lesbians who are alienated from 'society' on two levels. Although I think there are inherent problems of definition here related to *perceived* and *real* social threats (it is too easy for heterosexuals to dismiss acts of homophobia as 'imaginary'[14]), I think Modleski's model has some compatibility with certain reading strategies in this instance too. Crime fiction is a site for the expression of anxieties about society, and the appeasement of that fear,[15] is structurally inscribed in the narrative. As the paranoid's fears are projected onto a perceived 'enemy', a primary psychoanalytic scene is being replayed. Modleski invokes W W Meissner[16] in describing how, within the process of individuation, the child defines itself through opposition. The need for an enemy, therefore, may be a necessary step towards a conception of self as a separate identity.

While in the crime novel, the enemy is named and destroyed, in the lesbian crime novel the terms are often effectively inverted so that the state becomes the site of (paranoidal?) fears and the sleuth the representative of the 'other', and usually, the victor. The resolution is achieved in two stages; firstly through self-determination (a process of individuation essential to the thriller mode,[17] and secondly through integration and communality, features shared by most lesbian novels. The first phase is often represented by 'coming out', the second by finding a lover (romance), or the lesbian community (politicisation). The protagonists deal with fear and paranoia through action, by becoming active agents of their own destiny. The formation of identity happens through the solution of a crime. The central narrative device and locus of readerly pleasure is *discovery*.

Suspense, in the crime novel, derives from adopting the perspective associated primarily with an individual, who is the source and arbiter of our pleasure. At a simplistic level, what happens to her happens to us, whilst we 'suspend' our disbelief. Within the fictional world of the crime novel all appearances are ambiguous, the protagonist is the sole repository for our trust, a lone stable point surrounded by chaos. In four of these novels, *Mrs Porter's Letter*[18] and *The Burnton Widows*[19] by Vicki P McConnell, and *Murder in the Collective*[20] and *Sisters of the Road*[21] by Barbara Wilson – which are as much concerned with the process of becoming a lesbian as with the solution of a mystery – the text posits lesbianism as a strategy for dealing with evil and disruption. Lesbianism is depicted as an inner natural state lying dormant and waiting to be discovered. It is a beacon of authenticity in a perverse and fragmented society. This notion of a core of human nature, untouched and unpolluted by society is in the idealist tradition of Reich and Fromm, and relates to the enduring myth of sex as being the repository of secret and profound truth in the individual's soul, or centre. The opposition authentic lesbianism/inauthentic heterosexuality has been identified in such early novels as Rita Mae Brown's *Rubyfruit Jungle* (1973)[22], and continues to structure many lesbian novels of 'self-discovery'. The premise that there is a 'self' to discover is problematic. Invoking a concept of a fixed, stable, natural essence forming the truth of our identity is politically naive for lesbians, as this argument is always used more efficaciously against us in support of heterosexuality. It can also be employed to differentiate between 'real' (authentic) lesbians and 'political' (inauthenticate) lesbians, a redundant division if ever there was one. However, an attempt to invert the terms of the 'given' is still one significant step in the process of resistance, provoking some cultural struggle over definition. This inversion is an instance of what Foucault would describe as 'reverse discourse'.[23] According to Foucault discourses are constituted by power. Legitimate or 'true' discourse can be visualised as an area that is bound by lines of force asserting a particular ordering of the world as dominant. True discourse defines two things: firstly, what is within the 'realm of truth', and secondly, the difference between truth and untruth. Thus, in the discourse of heterosexism, a 'true' answer to the question 'What caused her to be a lesbian?' would be framed in terms of her sin, sickness or failed heterosexuality; an answer in terms of her childhood obsession with mashed potatoes would be considered 'untrue'. Outside the lines of forces of the discourse is the area of illegitimacy, of alternative – and thus subversive – utterances. These lie not within truth/untruth, but in 'fiction'. For example, Adrienne Rich's notion of 'Compulsory Heterosexuality'[24] would fall outside the realm of truth because its very terms are not recognised as legitimate. In other words, it is a fiction.

But Adrienne Rich's approach is also problematic. It is part of a reverse discourse which posits a notion of a transhistorical subject ('lesbian') in competion with the legitimate (heterosexual) view of subjectivity.

True discourse is, in a more 'literal' sense, upheld by its own Fictions; in mainstream crime fiction, by the end of the novel, the detective hero has re-formed the state by imposing order on disruption. Thus if traditional crime fiction is seen as 'true discourse' or even 'true Fiction', then we must ask whether lesbian crime fiction is an illegitimate and subversive utterance. According to Foucault true discourses construct subjectivities. If lesbian crime fiction offers alternative constructions of subjectivity, is it in fact subversive? What are the alternative constructions of subjectivity it posits?[25]

Mrs Porter's Letter genuflects in the direction of generic homogeneity with its muscle-bound hoods, plotting patriarchs, prostitutes and plane-hopping, but essentially the crime is peripheral; the real purpose of this rootless Denver-based pulp is mystic revelation. Nyla Wade is eight weeks divorced, a hack journalist with an inner spirit named 'Woman Writer'(p.8). Through the acquisition of an antique desk from a gothic junk shop she finds some old love letters and proceeds, by circuitous means, to find and return them to the (secret) sender. The purple prose contained therein renews in Nyla some kind of romantic idealism, a cure for her own steely cynicism. When finally the ardent author, W Stone, is discovered, 'he', is shockingly a 'she', and the closetry is explained. Except that, given the enthusiastic over use of the male pronoun everytime W Stone is mentioned, and the subtitle *A Lesbian Mystery* most readers would guess this at an early stage. The recipient of these lavender love-lines is a Cybil Porter, who stamps her psychic hologram on the subconscious of Ms Wade in the form of a pulsating orchid, which appears at points of (dramatic) climax to indicate her metaphysical presence. These implausible emanations are perhaps the visible extension of that ubiquitous investigative talent: intuition.

Mrs Porter's Letter contains some hilariously clichéd moments, and it is difficult to tell if they are intended as elevated satire, or better still, serious realism. Ms Wade's search for the missing lover, W Stone, is of course symbolic; she discovers tough prostitute Sara, ('... her black eyes a maelstrom of mystery' p.147) who functions as the prompter to Ms Wade's proto-lesbianism. There follows the near-obligatory bathroom mirror scene (remember *Lianna*?) in which Nyla probes her deepest self, discovers the potential for 'that syncopation of body and mind' only two women could share, and declares 'Yes, I'm probably a lesbian' (p.162). This personal revelation seems somewhat precipitous. Despite her apparent feminism, and therefore, one would expect, an awareness of the political dimensions involved, after one conversation with the woman, she is in love and ready to give up her previous heterosexuality – dormant thought it may be.

Nevertheless, this is romance not realism; instantly Nyla is admitted to the secret club of dykedom: a new colleague with a certain 'way of standing' (p.180) gives Nyla a knowing smile:

> As I put my hand out to shake hers, I wondered what kind of sign I was wearing that I didn't have on before. Something she saw and read and wanted me to understand ... we were two strong women just a little different from everyone around us ... I had been recognised only a few hours after I had recognised myself. (p.181)

As Nyla enters the private mystic communion of lesbianism, the reader is inculcated into the pleasures of recognition, transformation and privilege. In the final homily she describes the social prejudice this will entail, but in some epicentral space 'I have Sara within me, Sheila and Yolanda, Betts Wattle, and now, too, Cybil and Winona' (p.209). This could be a radical assertion of the collective subject. But I propose this tentatively since lesbianism is also deemed a 'part of nature', a biological rationale excluding political or cultural influences.

The Burnton Widows capers along in a similar mode, Nyla Wade having moved to Oregon enticed from Denver by a job at the *Burnton Beckoner*. A piece of local lesbian history, a gothic castle overlooking Burnton, a family seat of pioneer matriarch Druscilla Ketcham, and scene of a recent gruesome murder, is under threat from property developers. Largely through the effort of bent connections Nyla Wade re-solves the murders of two lesbian lovers, Joan and Valerie, who were butchered in their beds. The connectedness of the gay community is stressed, and indeed, Nyla's detection is reliant on its independent information and skills. This is a communal investigation initiated by subcultural loyalties.

The gays and lesbians in Burnton are self-consciously 'other' to the town, and in the end it is the town itself which is implicated in the form of the local fraternal demagogy, financial corruption tainting all ranks up to the Mayor. The main social fabric becomes the harbinger of

criminality, the gay community the repository of moral
outrage. This is a neat inversion of the lesbian/gay
stereotype 'sick pervert', the (as yet undiscovered)
murderer handles a copy of *Frankenstein* covetously at the
scene of crime, and, a year later this voyeuristic sadist is
hailed as a 'first rate monster' (p.239); he is, significantly,
a lawyer.[26]

The novel opens and closes with a love story, and
continually the references flow as to the parallel nature of
the two relationships, the first, the murdered Joan and
Valerie, the second their avengers, Nyla and Lucy. *The
Burnton Widows* is clearly a lesbian romance, but with a
spiritual edge similar to *Mrs Porter's Letter*. The ghosts of
Valerie and Joan communicate with similar mystic
messages, seeming to murmur from walls or with the
movement of the sea. It is as though the imposed
categorisation 'other' has become internalised and
projected into 'otherworldly', and the desire to legitimate a
universal lesbian spirituality, a panacea, maybe, for real
lesbian loneliness and isolation. This sense of cosmic
communality is pleasantly romantic but glosses over the
many political facets of subjectivity and difference. The
tendency to label a particular cultural experience as
paradigmatic has been severely and rightfully criticised by
the many black/disabled/lesbian/working class women in
the women's movement. Too often an attempt to articulate
a group's identity becomes spoken by those with the most
powerful voice, the desire to unite coming at the expense
of the differently oppressed.

Both these books make light-duty but pleasurable
reading, they are in the best tradition of pulp fiction and
should be enjoyed as such. The key narrative movement is,
as aforementioned, self-discovery followed by integration
into *communitas*. I think I enjoyed them particularly
because they provided a *break* from the unmitigating and
worthy 'social realism' of the more overtly feminist texts. It
is not necessarily the case, however, that the latter will
place the self 'in process', problematising identity as a
healthily unstable state. Rebecca O'Rourke's *Jumping the
Cracks*[27], for example, doesn't particularly focus on

subjectivity, but remains a well-crafted acerbic social criticism of Thatcher's divided Britain. But there are texts which combine both concerns. In *Murder in the Collective* by Barbara Wilson we meet Pam Nilson, thinly disguised Proto-Dyke. Her hands sweat and her body is wracked by erotic fevers as she gulps and swallows in the presence of Hadley; they do manage to consummate their lust, the romantic tension yoked to the crime fictional hermeneutic of alternate disclosure and disappointment. Wilson is crafty, romantic closure is superceded by a morass of familiar complexity: Elena loves Fran but Fran loves Hadley, Pam loves Hadley but Hadley loves Fran. Pam's new identity gives her individuation through a sense of difference, a political structure reinforced by the text in its dialectical oppositions lesbian/heterosexual, Black/white, poor/rich. The novel problematises meaning by constantly undermining textual and social conventions; things are never what they seem. 'Identity' is seen as a transitional process of discovery involving contradictory states of desire. Pam moves through a panopoly of revulsion and fear, guarded prejudice, nervous involvement, romantic idealism, crunching self-doubt, and finally perhaps, realism: 'Lesbians were no better than anyone else' (p.164). The overall movement is towards inclusion into a kind of heterogeneous plurality and tolerance.

In *Sisters of the Road* Wilson plays with several forms and ideas first explored in *Murder in the Collective*. The thriller structure provides a coathanger on which to support her politics. Wilson confronts the reader with sexual crime through a narrative process in which we become more and more embroiled in child prostitution and sexual abuse, so much so that in the final denouement the distancing frame them/us breaks down when the sleuth herself is violently raped by the murderer. *Sisters of the Road* sets out to destroy some of the vicariousness of crime fiction – this is no comfortable fantasy. Initially Pam Nilsen almost sidles off the page in self-depreciation, she is indecisive, doubtful, unfit, afraid of heights, and sits on conscience-stricken ideological fences. Pam Nilsen *looks* 'with an anthropologist's eye', but this gaze has no power to change: 'There were things here I needed to feel as well as witness' (p.53). Pam's emotional involvement increases with her growing self-knowledge, as an individual and as a lesbian, both resulting in more power to act. The message is also for the reader; we cannot just observe sexual crime and have pity for the victim as 'other'. The perpetrators are the actual and symbolic Father, brother, the site of struggle is the family, and the injured are ourselves.

This is a recurring theme in lesbian crime fiction; I want to know what is the symbolic and psychoanalytic import of 'murdering our fathers'? To retrieve that ideal and perfect union with our mothers perhaps ... is this why I'm reading these books? As I have not myself entirely come to grips with the complexity of this interpretation, I can only gesture towards its significance. It is an attempt to recover the pre-oedipal state of self-in-relation to the mother, a mutually beneficial symbiosis ideally constructed as warm, safe, and loving. It reminds us of our crucial interdependence with (and therefore responsibility to) others, destabilising patriarchal attitudes such as individualism and competitiveness. Julia Kristeva[28] names the pre-linguistic play of communication between the mother and the child 'semiotic'. It has the power to disrupt the 'iron grip' of the masculine control of language and therefore meaning production itself. These are only two brief ideas concerning the implications of 'murdering our fathers'.

In the last ten pages Pam becomes human as her voyeuristic posturing is discarded and replaced by real, felt, lived experience. As we surmised all along, '... it was my own life I wanted to change' (p.158). I would suggest that this has another more literary symbolism: the detective hero, unified and reified, can only offer us limited identification and political usefulness; his 'objectivity' is an imposed masculinised form upon the feminist sleuth. The book points out both the complexities and the power lying in shared oppression and multiple subjectivities:

I felt that whatever had made Pam a person, whatever I knew or had known about myself was being crushed out of me, was spinning into fragments like a planet smashed by meteors. (p.194)

In a clever reversal of roles it is Trish (the 'victim') who picks her up, dusts her off, and stops her acting like a 'crushed grape' (p.200). Here, again, we experience the importance of seeing the self in relation to others, us in them, and them in us. This is all a far cry from Arthur Conan Doyle's archetypal Holmes, a 'Nietzschean superior man ... a man immune from human weakness and passions',[29] a man who is essentially invulnerable. Holmes exalts rationality and intellect, and Doyle intended him to be a model to all young men of his time. Feminist fiction has progressed from the 1970s when providing strong powerful role models was a political necessity. Strategic though this was, and is, as Elizabeth Wilson points out it has a limited use:

> ... however good it is to be strong, we feel ambivalent about the strong, powerful woman, since this [too] is an image that allows for no moment of weakness, and cannot reflect the diversity and complexity of our desires ... This is a form of romanticism.[30]

Sisters of the Road problematises lesbian identity and romance. A seemingly straightforward flirtation between Pam and Best Printing colleague Carole progresses towards the conventional sexual encounter intrinsic to the thriller. But Pam is misreading the signs, Carole isn't interested, and the reader's romantic fantasy is unseated by a further (too real) irony – Carole's new lover is Pam's immediate 'ex': 'Oh ... she said she knew you slightly.' (p.180). The difficulties of romance are treated with self-reflexive humour, and laughter subverts our own misplaced fantasies in a way which also leaves us feeling supported: we're not lost in the sexual labyrinth on our own.

The Sophie Horowitz Story by Sarah Schulman[31] takes a metafictional stroll through the field of lesbian crime fiction. The cover depicts two women's heads, looking like a mirror-image, engrossed in a passionate open-mouthed pre-kiss which looks on both sides like an attempted swallow; it prefigures a lot. Sophie smokes fourteen

different types of cigarettes and spends a great deal of the
narrative in oral pursuits.[32] Sophie Horowitz is a Jewish
journalist in the ubiquitous feminist collective, this time
Feminist News. The novel is set firmly in lower eastside
Manhattan. The characters are an amalgam of day-glo
stereotypes, luridly satiric, ranging diversely from the
court-room to the sewer. The social criticism succeeds
primarily through style, this is literary *camp*, it is
ostentatious, extravagantly absurd, a parodic undercutting
of both hegemonic and radical sacred cows. The reader's
attempt to 'make sense' is continually being usurped; the
expected meaning develops only to be turned back on
itself, semantic slippage and non-signification highlights
the futility of denotation. In the search for Laura Wolfe
Sophie is shown an old photograph by her contemporary
Vivian:

> This is me and Laura at a demonstration in Washington
> Square Park. Look, we are both wearing flowers in our hair.
> The woman over there turned out to be a police agent. The
> other woman in the back, she was killed by the National
> Guard ... Sometimes when it feels like a dream I try to figure
> it out. Then I realise it's too complicated to understand.
> That's how I know it's real life. (p.124-5)

An image of 70s political romanticism, of 'flower power',
disguises violence and deception; things are not what they
seem, and a safe strategy is to accept ambiguity and
confusion. Sophie is continually falling for women who
appear to be something they are not: Germaine, Laura,
Vivian and Eva represent aspects of Sophie's desire, but
she creates them as such, and the ascribed meaning is
consistently mistaken. Sophie does not, and cannot, read
the signs. Significantly, the one sex scene in the book takes
place behind the synagogue curtain with an aptly named
photographer, 'Muffin'. Despite the picturesque subversion the act is cut short by them overhearing the men of
the Torah – the book of the Law – conclude their service
and preclude the women's sexual satisfaction.
My readerly expectations were confounded on two

generic levels – romance and crime fiction – which created an emotional elasticity: I must comply with the ironic distance, and question my own investment in formulaic satisfaction. The pleasure relies on my intertextual awareness: the construction of romantic desire and its concomitant frustration is a familiar literary form, and similarly the search for a personal archetype. The disruption of meaning brings the instability of the form itself to light; the detective story's insistence on factual truth falls into ambiguity and contradiction. The sleuth continuously misreads the clues. Into a markedly serious, straight-laced genre the author transfuses play, bringing to my notice the text's artifice, calling attention to the literary and ideological confluence of crime fiction with 'the real'. Crime fiction texts constantly assure the reader of their mimetic function through continued reference to actual places, dates, people, and organisations. Part of the pleasure of reading depends on this sense of authenticity, allowing me to experience normally inaccessible or forbidden activities. So, I can, for a moment, be Detective Kate Delafield of the Los Angeles Police Department beating the shit out of a potential rapist on a gay-bashing spree (*Murder at the Nightwood Bar* chapter 10). But this is precisely my point: this scenario is highly unlikely (one lone policewoman taking on three stoned and homophobic youths armed with pipes ... and winning), and is merely an expedient exchange of one type of perceived 'reality' for another. Lesbian crime fiction provides a site of struggle over definitions, positing the lesbian at the centre of meaning dissemination.

The Sophie Horowitz Story is a parody of 'types'; their ascribed meanings, however, are constantly shifting and inverting: the terrorist is a nun, the District Attorney a fence, the respected journalist an S/M cokehead, the winos FBI agents, the radical lawyer an avaricious status-seeker. The stereotypes derive from both the dominant and alternative cultural arena. The novel is, in part, a reaction against lesbian feminist prescriptivity, offering an incisive caricature:

> [Laura Wolfe] ... was part of a group known as Women
> Against Bad Things. They had some kind of politics which
> none of us understood. Whatever we did, they didn't like it
> and usually picketed feminist events with very long leaflets.
> (p.5)

It reflects political maturation that feminists can parody
their own excesses. The only stable point in this satirical
onslaught is Sophie. In her ironic humour she distances
herself (and us) from the semantic cacophony. Mrs
Noseworthy, Sophie's neighbour, turns out to be the
famous detective author 'King James'. Grey-haired Mrs
Noseworthy sits quietly in her rocking chair stroking her
cat and analysing evidence, an aggregate Marple/Pym/
Silver contemporised with an incongruous lavender
BMW, a homosexual popsinger son, and titles such as
Murder in the Missionary Position. She comments on the
progress of the investigation, Sophie's part in it and her
credibility as a detective hero, interprets the clues, and
finally alerts the police 'in my best Italian accent' (p.136).
In metafiction identity is foregrounded, (Sophie is looking
for Laura, and looking for 'herself', the pleasure derives
from the recognition not of selfhood but of roles.
Schulman deploys metafictional frames to obfuscate these
binaries self/roles, truth/fiction (or even true Fiction/
fiction!).

   Traditional detective fiction is a highly formalised and
predictable genre offering pleasure and release of tension
through the affirmation of received and uncontested
meanings. For the Jewish/feminist/lesbian reader there is
some pleasurable complicity with the text in its representation of familiar (sub)cultural signs. However, the reader
becomes disconcerted as these are undermined by parody.
The reader's resultant unease reflects her more realistic
social positioning, and allows expression to the constant,
unconscious shifting of roles/selves necessary for social
interaction. By seeing what she is, what she is not, and
what she could be, we are reminded of the 'up' side of
complex subjectivity.

   In examining these novels I thought I would be able to

extrapolate a tidy and cohesive theory about why I read them, but the reasons are more complex than I allowed. It is clear they are concerned with lesbian identity and subjectivity, a controversial area which is explored pleasurably by employing a narrative process of 'discovery'. Thus, the reader reads to discover 'herself', but also to reconstruct 'herself' as a woman empowered and centred. The novels offer a fantasy of control, and so radically invert the real relations of her oppression.

Part of the attraction of crime fiction is that it offers the reader security and an affirmation of her values. By placing her in the centre of the narrative she becomes the site of meaning production. Psychoanalytically oriented reader response critic Norman Holland holds that 'interpretation is a function of identity',[33] and that we find in a text that which we are predisposed to fear or wish for. Because I am grieving I am also reading and grieving. Thus, in both lesbian and traditional crime fiction I am comforted: into the fictional realm of fear and chaos steps a figure of order and resolution. That figure allays my fears for the moment of reading. But this resolution is temporal; thus I must read again and again. Once I know who the murderer is, I cannot read the book and fear, so that crucial cathartic release is denied.

This is my personal story of reading,[34] but because I am also constructed by that reverse discourse 'lesbianism', I share this reading, in part, with thousands of 'others'. We are all heras, successfully overcoming textual obstacles in the achievement of our quests for meaning and self-realisation. In itself this is a political act: to be a lesbian is to undermine the hegemony of heterosexuality. The dominant discourse has incorporated ways of continually asserting its superiority by the hierarchical ordering of the opposition heterosexual/homosexual, and by the negation of homosexuality, as in 'I'm not queer'. To assert lesbianism visibly, as a healthy and positive sexuality, is strategically vital, especially since we are in the shadow of growing homophobia within an increasingly reactionary political climate. We must however, go further than simply proposing alternative unified subjects in opposition to hegemonic discourse. We must deconstruct the notion of subjectivity altogether. It is essential that we do not expediently substitute political strategy for a critical self analysis. For example, because heterosexism exists, this does not mean that all expressions of lesbianism are progressive.

During the 1970s lesbian identity was intricately tied to protest; during the 1980s we seem to be fighting our street battles at home with lesbian detective stories which, if section 28 of the Local Government Act succeeds, we won't have got from our local library. Stories of reading can, however, invoke communality in themselves. Lesbians have historically always looked to fiction in order to understand their sexuality. I can distinctly recall one long hot summer in Weymouth sunbathing on the beach and reading book after book after book. I had discovered feminism and lesbianism together, in fiction, and I couldn't read enough. The guilty excitement I experienced, I was sure, was written all over my face. Whether it was through a process of recognition or reconstruction, I was seeing myself in these narratives. You don't, however, have to 'come out' to a book, so it's a safe arena in which to explore. Because of the importance of fiction to lesbians, novels continue to be points of communication and discussion between women. We all have stories of reading to tell.

I want to talk about one more book, and ask why it has been such an uncompromising hit with the lesbian community that it almost stands as the referent for lesbian crime fiction: Mary Wings' *She Came Too Late*.[35] The text shies away from didacticism; political issues give the book a moral baseline, but 'story' re-emerges with primary importance. Emma Victor ('I'm a victor') works for Boston Women's Hotline, but is cured of political romanticism, '... it doesn't have any flash at all, just a kind of deadly dullness' (p.17). Issues raised include women and reproductive technology, high society vice and corruption, union busting, the tentative position of charitable organisations relying on private funding and the questionable alliances that that provokes; but these have relational, peripheral importance to the central fantasies of power and desire. Victor is a strong, independent woman in control of her chosen identity and lifestyle, 'life was streamlined and lonely and I was liking it that way' (p.13): she defines her own boundaries. When Dr Frances Cohen appears, 'A woman even my best fantasies couldn't touch' (p.6), the reader gets to enjoy that vicarious identification-pleasure as the romance ensues. Cohen is the mother/whore who will nurse you when sick, towel dry your hair, and turn up on your doorstep in her pyjamas. She is a repository of mystery, and, in the true crime tradition, is a suspect to the end. Our fears are allayed, she was merely perfecting lesbian frogs.

The sexual fantasy is overlaid with ambiguity – *She Came Too Late*, as the title would imply, is strewn with innuendo particular to lesbian sexual practice. This creates in the reader a kind of privileged confederacy, a legitimation of illicit pleasures. The text pushes out into an even greater sexual shadow: sadomasochism. The rationale for their constant battles for the 'upper hand' is strikingly similar to arguments put forward by SAMOIS:[36]

> love [was] made possible because the power devils had been admitted and therefore banished. (p.77)

Victor 'goes shopping' in lesbian bars, gets turned on by striptease, stomps around in black leather and slips from butch to femme. Frances Cohen has her boss 'on a leash' which she can tighten 'anytime I want' (p.111), has hips 'like two holsters hanging below her waist' (p.37), and likes power in bed:

> I felt her exploring my mouth, taking it, drawing me into her. I would have been afraid except that I felt her warm hand on my back ... She had my hands clasped over my head with one strong arm and her other hand went further and further pursuing the boundaries, taking me so far along in the excitement it was nearly pain ... I fought with the passivity but

it was only fun to fight it. I let her go wherever she wanted ...
(p.67)

This passivity is indulged because we know Emma Victor is
really a Strong Woman permitting her submission
fantasies (and ours?) a limited expression. However
pleasurable this proves to be, I am reminded of E Ann
Kaplan's cautionary:

> ... to simply celebrate whatever gives us sexual pleasure seems
> to be both problematic and too easy: we need to analyse how it
> is that certain things turn us on, how sexuality has been
> constructed in patriarchy to produce pleasure in the
> dominance-submission forms ...[37]

Much of the pleasure in *She Came Too Late* springs from its
sexual openness. This move away from the idealised
prescriptiveness of the 1970s involves dipping a toe into
murky waters. Throughout there is a sense of play, laying
bare the artifice of gender and subverting our own lesbian
dress-codes. Emma dons sheer black stockings, stilettoes
and a dress as part of a draggish disguise. The detailed
process of preparation and bedizenment is a private
familiar feminine ritual we complicitly enjoy, even to the
final twirl in the mirror: 'I saw it was good. I was a girl.'
(p.90). Emma Victor embodies and unifies the contradictions of gender; she is strong and soft, butch and
femme, offering diversity but not fragmentation.

Her ability to change subject position not only
foregrounds those positions but also provides the reader
with some vicarious resolution of the conflicting discourses
around sexuality. When Victor walks into 'The Yellow
Door' club on Mass Avenue and drops several whiskies she
is emulating the hard-boiled dick; she is approached
sexually by a man whom she peremptorily disposes of; she
watches a striptease depicted in voyeuristic detail. When
the stripper fixes her own eyes on Victor the power shifts:
'I watched her decide what to do with me' (p.180). As she
draws a phallic feather boa through her crotch she stares
at Victor, who is sexually stimulated. Victor's thoughts

move on to male punters and the politics of biological reproduction. As she sits she has passed through several different states of subjectivity, ultimately clearing her mind for action. It looks so easy.

Foucault has described how all discourses both constrain and construct us in that once we start naming ourselves we begin to fix meaning and prohibit flow.[38] On the other hand it is politically problematic for lesbians to relinquish these acts of naming and identification. Analysis of these novels has uncovered a certain unease around identity and subjectivity which seems to me to represent some, if limited, debate around sexuality. To take *She Came Too Late* for example: I am not proposing an equivalence between S/M and lesbian sexuality. I am saying that because lesbian sexuality is not fixed, should not be fixed, and does not operate beyond power relations,[39] we must not celebrate it uncritically, in word or in deed, but constantly critique it, and ourselves, as cultural subjects of diverse interlocking and conflicting discourses; fiction must be an important site for this struggle. By presenting us with alternative constructions of subjectivity our different desires can be explored.

Victor is strong but enjoys being made submissive. This paradox potentially undercuts the polarities of masculinity and femininity integral to romance; there are many other examples of subversion I could give. Conversely, the concomitant dependence on traditional notions of order, closure and reason, which situates many of these novels firmly within the dominant genre, offers me solace and security. These contradictions in the text mirror the contradictions in me. One fiction I offer you is the expression of my grief. It is no more or less intrinsic to me than is my lesbianism. They both appear as truth because the discourses, in their effectiveness, obscure their own mechanisms. As Jonathan Cook[40] has so pithily put it, 'Truth is the unrecognised fiction of a successful discourse'. He continues:

Instead of seeing the literary work as an ideal aesthetic harmony, or the equally ideal resolution of psychological tensions in the author or reader, discourse theory conceives of the literary work as an instance of the historically variable institutions of literature, an institution which mediates relations between writer and reader in different ways at different times, and in so doing, echoes, transforms, or challenges the uneven distribution of power within societies.[41]

Thus the need to be vigilant over all our fictions.

With thanks to Razia Aziz, without whom ...

Notes

[1] hera – I use this term in preference to heroine, which implies a diminutive hero.

[2] Robert E Skinner, *The Hard-Boiled Explicator: A Guide to the Study of Dashiell Hammet, Raymond Chandler and Ross Macdonald*, The Scarecrow Press, New Jersey and London 1985, p.2.

[3] See especially Michel Foucault, *Power/Knowledge: Selected Interviews and Other Writing 1972-1977*, Colin Gordon (ed), Harvester Press, Brighton 1980, and Michel Foucault *The History of Sexuality Volume 1: An Introduction*, Pelican 1981.

[4] Annette Kolodny, 'Dancing Through the Minefield: Some Observations on Theory, Practice and Politics of a Feminist Literary Criticism', in *Feminist Studies* 6, 1 (Spring) pp.1-25.

[5] For an example of this approach in literary criticism see Susan Koppelman Cornillon (ed), *Images of Women in Fiction: Feminist Perspectives*, Bowling Green State Popular Press, USA 1972.

[6] Katherine V Forrest, *Amateur City*, Pandora Press 1987.

[7] Katherine V Forrest, *Murder at the Nightwood Bar*, Pandora Press 1987.

[8] Catherine Stimpson, 'Zero Degree Deviancy: The Lesbian Novel in English', in Elizabeth Abel (ed), *Writing and Sexual Difference*, The Harvester Press, Brighton 1982, p.244.

[9] Havelock Ellis, 'Sexual Inversion', in *Studies in the Psychology of Sex*, New York, 1936, p.122, quoted in Stimpson, *op cit*, p.248.

[10] Catherine Belsey, *Critical Practice*, Methuen, London 1980, p.65.

[11] By depriving him of his human status, and according him an animal status, this excuses any amount of physical experimentation and abuse; this is the very hierarchy the Animal Rights Movement is at pains to critique. Moreover, the implicit conflation of 'animal' with 'evil' reveals a conceptual confusion on the nature of deviancy: an animal cannot be consciously malignant.

[12] This universality is implicitly Western and caucasian as the (racist) use of 'cannibal subspecies' suggests, evoking, as it does, an image of the African savage.

[13] Tania Modleski, *Loving with a Vengeance: Mass-Produced Fantasies for Women*, Methuen, New York 1984.

[14] For example the popular belief in the existence of a free and democratic Britain peopled by heterogenous equals effectively ignores lesbian and gay experiences of prejudice as an oppressed minority. It refuses to acknowledge the role of power in society and therefore acts to maintain the status quo. The lesbian/gay response to the many actual and feared instances of oppression in daily life is therefore ridiculed as paranoia by this commonsense attitude.

[15] As so cogently described in Jerry Palmer, *Thrillers: Genesis and Structure of a Popular Genre*, Edward Arnold, London 1978.

[16] William W Meissner, *The Paranoid Process*, Jason Aronson, New York 1978, p.767, quoted in Modleski *op cit* p.74.

[17] See Jerry Palmer, *op cit.*

[18] Vicki P McConnell, *Mrs Porter's Letter*, Naiad Press, USA 1984.

[19] Vicki P McConnell, *The Burnton Widows*, Naiad Press, USA 1982.

[20] Barbara Wilson, *Murder in the Collective*, The Women's Press, London 1984.

[21] Barbara Wilson, *Sisters of the Road*, The Women's press, London 1987.

[22] Jonathan Dollimore, 'The Dominant and the Deviant: A Violent Dialectic', in *Critical Quarterly* Vol 28 nos 1 and 2, Spring and Summer 1986, pp.179-192.

[23] To quote Sonja Ruehl in her article 'Radcliffe Hall and the Lesbian identity': 'Once a category like homosexuality has been set up and individuals have started to be defined by it, then the so-named 'homosexuals' may group under it and start to use it to speak for themselves. So, Foucault says, 'homosexuality began to speak on its own behalf ... often in the same vocabulary, using the same categories, by which it was medically disqualified'. He calls this process the development of a 'reverse discourse'. (Rosalind Brunt and Caroline Rowan (eds), *Feminism, Culture and Politics*, Lawrence and Wishart, London 1982, p.18).

It is a debatable point whether Foucault can be interpreted as positing a subject to liberate.

[24] Adrienne Rich, 'Compulsory Heterosexuality and Lesbian Existence', in Ann Snitow *et al* (eds), *Desire: The Politics of Sexuality*, Virago, London 1984, pp.212-241.

[25] To stretch the analogy, one can ask the same question of the relationship between lesbian-feminism and the dominant hegemonic discourse. To square the circle, one might also investigate in what ways if any lesbian crime fiction 'upholds' the politics of lesbian feminism(s).

[26] In several of these texts the binary heterosexual sickness/homosexual health is common, and relates back to themes in earlier novels such as *Rubyfruit Jungle*, as previously mentioned. For an interesting exposé of

the ideological conflation between sex, health, and sickness, see Frank
Mort, 'The Domain of the Sexual' in *Screen Education* 36 Autumn 1980
pp.69-84 and Lucy Bland 'The Domain of the Sexual: A Response' in
Screen Education 39 Summer 1981, pp.56-67.

[27] Rebecca O'Rouke, *Jumping the Cracks*, Virago 1987.

[28] See Ann Rosalind Jones, 'Inscribing Femininity: French Theories of
the Feminine', in Gayle Greene and Coppelia Kahn (eds), *Making A
Difference: French Literary Criticism*, Methuen, London 1985, pp.80-112.

[29] Julian Symons, *Bloody Murder*, Viking, London 1972, p.66.

[30] Elizabeth Wilson, *Mirror Writing: An Autobiography*, Virago, London
1982, p.155.

[31] Sarah Schulman, *The Sophie Horowitz Story*, Naiad Press, USA 1984.

[32] Caught in Pizza Hut playing Pac-Man with her brother, Sophie
observes: 'Suddenly Ms Pac-Man appears on the electric screen. She's in a
maze. She has to gobble up as many little blue dots as she can before the
monsters catch her. It's social-realism about women and over-eating'.
(p.67) It is a pertinent remark, the prevalence of food in the novel
metonymically asserts its Jewishness, but also provides a cultural reference point for all women preoccupied with the inevitable appropriation,
treatment, distribution and fetishism of food. Sophie's investigations are
punctuated not by bourbon or Black label, but blintzes, borscht and
bagels. Feminist fiction, like much women's fiction, is full of food (See
Joanna Russ 'Somebody's Trying to Kill Me and I Think It's My Husband: The Modern Gothic' in *Journal of Popular Culture* Vol 6 Spring
1973 Bowling Green University Ohio pp.666-691). Often, in lesbian
crime fiction, after a scene of narrative suspense, the sleuth cooks a
delicious meal which serves to placate the reader's tension, to 'normalise'
the fictional realm and to ensure continuing identification with the
protagonist.
     In keeping with its cover, *The Sophie Horowitz Story* opens with a
sentence about food and feeding. The story closes with a cigarette and a
figurative swallowing: as Sophie walks 'off into the skyline' (p.158) she is
sucked back into the city, the ultimate sign of culture.
     NB A further comment on oral pursuits; the detective story depends
on the gathering and dissemination of information through gossip, *aka*
'women's oral tradition'.

[33] Norman N Holland 'UNITY IDENTITY TEXT SELF' in *Proceedings
of the Modern Language Association*, 90, 1975, p.816, quoted in
Elizabeth Freund *The Return of the Reader: Reader Response Criticism*,
Methuen, London and New York 1987, p.124.

[34] 'To speak of the meaning of a work is to tell a story of reading'
Jonathan Culler, in *On Deconstruction: Theory and Criticism After Structuralism*, Cornell University Press, Ithaca 1982, p.35.

[35] Mary Wings, *She Came Too Late*, The Women's Press, London 1986.

[36] SAMOIS is a lesbian feminist S/M organisation based in San Francisco.

[37] E Ann Kaplan 'Is the Gaze Male' in Ann Snitow *et al* (eds), *Desire: The
Politics of Sexuality*, Virago, London 1984, p.328.

[38] See Michel Foucault, *The History of Sexuality Volume I: An Introduction*, *op
cit*.

[39] I do not subscribe to the romantic and essentialist notion that lesbianism is the meeting of two equals.

[40] In Roger Fowler (ed), *A Dictionary of Modern Critical Terms*, Routledge Kegan Paul, London 1987, p.64.

[41] *Ibid*, p.66.

Robots and Romance: The Science Fiction and Fantasy of Tanith Lee

SARAH LEFANU

Tanith Lee is a prolific and versatile writer of science fiction and fantasy who is better known in the USA than in the UK, although she was born here and has lived and worked in this country all her life. In this piece I am going to talk mainly about one of her science fiction novels, *The Silver Metal Lover*.[1] But first I would like to discuss some of her works of fantasy, for it is as a fantasy writer and most particularly as a writer of 'sword-and-sorcery' that she is best known.

Within a science fictional critical discourse fantasy does not necessarily denote the same kind of literature as it does in other fields of theory. Fantasy, and its sub-genre sword-and-sorcery, are categories used not just by theorists of science fiction, but by fans and readers too, to describe a literature that is distinct from, but overlaps with, science fiction. In science fiction bookshops science fiction and fantasy are sold side by side: readers tend to show a preference for one over the other, but will be aware of, and open to developments in either field. Science fiction and fantasy fans form a more active, more participatory readership than the readers of any other 'genre' fiction: there are countless self-published fanzines and regular conventions when readers, writers and others meet and mingle.

Rosemary Jackson,[2] who is a theorist of fantastic literature, stresses the subversive nature of fantasy, its interrogation of unitary ways of seeing, its tendency

121

towards the dissolution of structures and its open-endedness; theorists of science fiction, on the other hand, claim such potentially radical aims for science fiction, *not* for fantasy. But for Jackson science fiction is compensatory and transcendental. It offers a secular version of religious mythology, while Fantasy offers no such redemptory, recuperative powers, but instead dis-covers 'emptiness inside an apparently full reality'.[3]

Jackson contrasts fantasies with romances: 'Whereas fantasies (of dualism) by Mary Shelley, Dickens, Stevenson etc interrogate the cost of constructing an ego, thereby challenging the very formation of a symbolic cultural order, romances (of integration) by LeGuin, Lewis, White etc leave problems of social order untouched'.[4] Science fiction is, of course, heavily indebted to traditions of romance fiction but it is distinguished by its open-endedness – defined perhaps by the science fictional trope of the journey onwards and outwards (from a fictional, or relativistic centre) in an infinite, expanding universe. Such denial of limiting structures places it, too, within the traditions of fantastic narrative. Partisans of science fiction would refuse its exclusion from 'subversive' literature.[5] Indeed, Mary Shelley's Frankenstein which is accorded the status of subversive, fantastic literature, is more than any other Gothic text, claimed by science fiction as its own.

Fantasy, in the terminology of science fiction, usually denotes what Jackson calls 'faery'. It is used, on the whole, to describe a literature that is *not* open-ended, one, rather, that is nostalgic for a past order. In this article I will use the word 'fantasy' in its science fictional sense unless I state otherwise.

It might be useful to look at what practitioners and critics of science fiction have to say on the science fiction/fantasy distinction. Joanna Russ offers a working definition: fantasy has negative subjunctivity, it treats with what could not have happened. Science fiction allows what might happen, could happen, should happen, what might have happened (but didn't).[6] Science fiction, says Russ (drawing on Samuel Delany), expresses a tension between the possible and the impossible. Such a description of science fiction is not far removed from what Jackson calls 'the basic trope of fantasy', the oxymoron.

I have gone into this in some detail less to offer final definitions – and indeed the eclecticism of science fiction excludes such a possibility – as to give some sense of the different modes within which Tanith Lee works. Her writing draws on fantasy, 'faery' and science fiction, and contains a strong element of romance. I am not claiming that Lee's work is deeply radical but she has a wit and a subtlety that is brought to bear on the modes within which she writes with a result that is subversive both of readers' expectations and traditional narrative methods.

First, then sword-and-sorcery, which Tanith Lee goes in for in as full-blooded a way as any devotee of the literature could hope for. Sword-and-sorcery literature involves sword fights, magic spells, mighty-thewed blond heroes rescuing from slavery and a fate more titillating than death, slim-waisted, pointy-breasted princesses. It is a literature through which there runs a strong element of conservatism, a nostalgia for a 'natural' order, in which distinctions of gender, class and function are pre-ordained and rigidly adhered to. Any expression of sexuality is tramelled into traditional sex roles: males act and females react.

But sword-and-sorcery offers scope both for subversion and for humour, not least in the possibilities that sorcery offers for disguise, metamorphosis and the blurring of distinctions between what is constructed as separate. Lee is not the only writer to explore such possibilities; other writers like Joanna Russ and Fritz Leiber (both, like Lee, writers of science fiction as well as fantasy) are artful practitioners of the genre.

Even in her more traditionally structured sword-and-sorcery works, the epics *The Birthgrave*,[7] *The Storm Lord*[8] and their sequels, which tend to present a polarised view of the world based on particular archetypal notions of female and male; female as mystic, sensitive, intuitive; male as strong, active, public; even in these Lee pushes against the constraints of the form. But it is in works like *Cyrion*,[9] the novella *Sirriamnis*[10] and the 'Flat Earth'[11] series, in all of which sorcery is foregrounded over sword-fighting, that the subversive potential of the genre is most apparent.

Yet the rigid formula of sword-and-sorcery does offer its own possibilities for self-interrogation, and I think it is worth mentioning here Lee's foray into the Amazon story, a particular sub-genre of sword-and-sorcery, in which the maidens may still be pointy-breasted but are also mighty-thewed. Despite claims made by publishers and some writers (usually male) for the feminist nature of these stories (their science fictional equivalents are marvellously satirised by Joanna Russ in her story 'The Clichés from Outer Space'),[12] they only rarely challenge the rigid sexual stereotyping that provides the structural backbone of sword and sorcery.

Jessica Amanda Salmonson, in the introduction to *Amazons!*, goes so far as to say that 'the very act of women taking up sword and shield, to a society like our own which is ruled predominantly by men, is an act of revolution, whether performed in fact or in art'.[13] High claims, and would that it were so! But I would contend that swapping roles, having your heroines act as your heroes, does not necessarily challenge the roles themselves. Sexual role reversal is used for polemical purposes and so serves different functions for the women and men who employ it. In male writers it functions to express fears of the powerful, castrating m/other or, as Susan Wood put it, 'the underlying current of fear and hatred', played out in stories whose basic assumption 'seems to be that women who gain power will not want equality, but will, rather, destroy men as revenge for thousands of years of male oppression'.[14] In stories by women, role reversal can be used as a means of presenting strong, active images of women and of challenging women's inferior status both in the literature (sword-and-sorcery and science fiction) and, as Salmonson states, in 'fact'. Yet the swapping of roles offers only the very limited opportunity to replace one fixed stereotype with another. Unlike narratives which deal with metamorphosis and disguise, which challenge difference and notions of 'oppositeness', role reversal stories, despite, in many cases, a progressive if not a feminist aim, tend to corroborate gender differentiation. This, I think, is why novels like Marion Zimmer Bradley's *The Ruins of Isis*[15] and Gerd Brandenberg's *The Daughters of Egalia*[16] are so disappointing.

This is not to say that the Amazon stories do not pose a challenge, simply that that challenge is necessarily limited if it is not extended to the conventions within which the sexual stereotyping is placed. Which brings me to Tanith Lee's Amazon story, 'Northern Chess'[17] which does, I think, challenge those conventions; partly indeed, simply through her tough and delightful heroine, but more importantly by bringing into the never-never land of sword-and-sorcery a breath of sexual politics from a world outside it.

The story opens as Jaisel plods through a northern landscape of bare trees and monotonous grassless hills, her horse having collapsed and died under her fifteen miles back. She is always on the move, fleeing from the improverished and restricted existence imposed on women in this feudal/faery fantasy world, from the women she sees 'at their looms or in their greasy kitchens, or tangled with babies, or broken with field work, or leering out of painted masks from shadowy town doorways'. She is also fleeing from the law, from certain death by hanging and quartering, for having killed two footpads, one of whom has turned out to be a local petty lord out indulging himself in robbery and rape. This is a land 'for sad songs and dismal rememberings, and, when the night came, for nightmares and hallucinations'. It is gloriously gothic, rich with intimations of sorcery and devilment.

Jaisel, like Joanna Russ's Alyx, lives by her wits and her swords. Like Alyx, too, she is a thoroughly modern heroine, ideologically light years in advance of the fantasy world she inhabits. She looks androgynous: she is blonde, slim, attired in chain mail and has a gold sickle moon dangling from her left ear. When she meets two knights, they think at first that she is a boy and are suitably shocked to discover she is not. One of the knights, Renier, is at once on the defensive, suggesting that she should be sent back

to her father, husband and children. In the battle of wits
that follows, Jaisel is the winner. The two knights explain
what they are doing there – laying siege to the last
remaining castle of the alchemist and necromancer
Maudras, who was burned to death the previous year, but
whose curse still lies heavy on the land – and take her back
to the camp. On the way Renier warns her that because of
low morale, sickness amongst all the women, and the
general ghastliness of living under a curse, the knights
have lost their honour and are likely to rape her.

Readers unfamiliar with the conventions of sword-and-
sorcery may be surprised that the threat of rape is a
common topic of conversation amongst characters in the
genre: it functions, perhaps, as a metaphor for
masculinity, and serves as a means of keeping sexual
order. Jaisel's reply to Renier's statement, 'But probably
you have been raped frequently', is in the best Amazonian
tradition:

> 'Once', she said, 'ten years back. I was his last pleasure. I dug
> his grave myself, being respectful of the dead'. She met
> Renier's eyes again and added gently, 'and when I am in the
> district I visit his grave and spit on it'.[18]

Three assaults have been made on the castle of
Maudras. Knights and men have either been hideously
killed by invisible weapons, or have entered the castle and
never been seen again. No sign of life is visible inside the
castle. It is defended by sorcery. Over red wine and red
meat in the red pavilion, Renier starts babbling of the
honour of men, and insults Jaisel who has suggested they
should all give up and go home. She accuses him of being
drunk, and offers him more wine, slowly pouring the
contents of her goblet over his head. At once he leaps to
his feet and rides off to Maudras' castle, his manhood
shamed. The gates open to receive him. Jaisel follows later
that night, for she too has a sense of honour. She climbs
the castle walls and is immediately met with invisible
javelot bolts, hundreds of invisible sword blades, and
putrefying corpses that glow in the dark and light up the

inscriptions carved into the stones next to them, 'Maudras slew me'. But Jaisel is not a heroine for nothing. She feints, fights, finds Renier not quite dead, but is nearly overwhelmed by terror and exhaustion. Just as she thinks she will not survive, the onslaught ceases; the hideous ghostly face of the burned Maudras seems to glimmer before her, directing her to look at the inscription on the stone block against which she leans.

The denouement of the story relies on the kind of riddle that befogged Macbeth: the literal meaning of words is ignored in favour of consensus opinion (in *Macbeth* that woods can't move and that all men are born of women). So here, the curse that afflicts the castle, and has caused the death of countless knights, uses 'man' in its generic sense; taken literally, it does not affect women. Inscribed on the stone block, the curse reads: 'I, Maudras, to this castle do allot my everlasting bane, that no man shall ever approach its walls without hurt, nor enter it and live long. Nor, to the world's ending, shall it be taken by any man'. The joke is turned not just against those who assume 'woman' within 'man' but also against the conventions of sword-and-sorcery narratives, in which it is generally unquestioned that a curse against 'man' is, precisely, a curse against man (women being beneath contempt and curses). It undermines the position of the stock sword-and-sorcery characters: the powerful wily sorcerer is shown up as a fool for so underestimating the power of women, while the knights are mocked for their empty threats of rape and their empty notions of manhood and honour. Renier, the knight who has courted death to avoid shame, and who has been saved from the first if not the second by our heroine, asks sulkily, 'How many other prophecies could be undone, do you judge, Lady Insolence, that dismiss women in such a fashion?' 'As many as there are stars in heaven', replies Jaisel.

The success of this story lies partly in the elegance with which Tanith Lee constructs the sword-and-sorcery setting. For it is, finally, a tale of sword-and-sorcery rather than a pastiche of one. So, the 'fantastic' (in Jackson's sense) possibilities of its central trope, the death-in-life which the land suffers, are not denied. At the same time however Lee exploits the formulaic nature of the genre to introduce a level of ironic interrogation, one which questions the place of women not just within the genre but within a more general male-defined linguistic order.

But sword-and-sorcery does have its limits, and in general I find her works of fantasy more interesting. As I mentioned earlier these include *Cyrion*, *Sirriamnis* and the 'Flat Earth' series. Here the recurrence of female and male figures that correspond to the Jungian archetypes of anima and animus (common throughout Lee's work) is most strongly offset by the centrality of the themes of transformation and metamorphosis. (Her archetypal vein can be seen at its crudest in such works as *East of Midnight*,[19] in which the women's culture – moon-identified, shadowy, most powerful at night – is destroyed by yellow-haired, sun-identified males, who force the women, by a mixture of trickery and sexual manipulation, to abandon their cruel superstitions in favour of a rational 'modern' society.

Vampires, humans, dead, undead, female and male constantly meet and mingle. Lee's heroes and heroines are masters and mistresses of disguise, and none more so than Azhrarn, Lord of Darkness, Prince of Demons, protagonist, and indeed tragic hero, of the 'Flat Earth' series: tales of this earth and the under-earth set in a mythical time of pre-history before the world was round.

These works stand out amongst Lee's works of fantasy for the richness of their texture and the humour of both conception and execution. Their protagonists are, nominally, three of the Lords of Darkness: Azhrarn, Prince of Demons, Uhlume, Lord of Death and Chuz, Prince of Madness, but it is Azhrarn who is the undoubted hero of the three books, almost, one feels, despite the author's attempts in the second and third books to relegate him to the background. Of all Lee's transformations this is perhaps the boldest: Azhrarn, Lord of Demons, Satan, Lucifer, is tranformed into the figure of Christ in a scene of remarkable visual power, when he is impaled upon the rays of the rising sun, sacrificing himself, when the gods of upperearth have proved themselves indifferent to the fate of humankind, to save the human race, without whom, as Lucifer, his existence has no significance.

Unlike much fantasy writing there is no heterosexual norm. Azhrarn, the demon lover, is imbued with great erotic power, and ensnares both women and men and, indeed, at least one who is both. Simmu, in *Death's Master*, is alternately woman and man. S/he is, too, the issue of a *post mortem* (on the father's side) union. Sex is treated with a kind of reverent irreverence. Just as the physical laws of the 'real' world are broken, so are the cultural laws that forbid the union of sister and brother, of beast and human, of living and dead. As magical metamorphosis can challenge the notion of character as fixed or internally coherent, so a world of sexual disorder is uncovered by means of devilish disguise and trickery. When nothing is what it seems on what can a sexual morality be built?

In her science fiction, too, Tanith Lee likes to explore the possibilities of disguise. In *Don't Bite the Sun* and its sequel *Drinking Sapphire Wine*,[20] the long-term teen-aged protagonists while away their pleasure-filled days by regularly changing bodies. The heroine ('predominantly female'), who thinks a child might solve her problems of angst, tries to hoodwink the benevolently dictatorial authorities by offering her own sperm from a previous, male incarnation. Part of the fun of sexual relationships lies in keeping your partner guessing as to 'who' you are. Most disturbing of all for our heroine is the lover who turns up in one of her own favourite bodies. The erotic possibilities of disguise, whether in magical or science fictional form, recur throughout Lee's work.

Disguise is an important element in the novel I now want to talk about, although 'Who is Silver, what is he?' is a question to which I think readers will bring different answers.

The Silver Metal Lover was the first of Tanith Lee's novels that I read, and of her science fiction novels it remains my favourite. The plot follows that of a thousand romantic novels: poor little rich girl Jane, bullied by her tough successful mother and stuck in permanent adolescence,

mopes around her luxury house with a full heart and
no-one to whom she can pour it out. The road to
independence and adulthood lies through finding, and
keeping, the love of a good man. This, Jane partly
achieves; she is awakened to her own potentialities, sexual
and otherwise (her musical skill, for example, of which she
had been unaware, can be put to good use in earning a
living). But, tragically, she loses her lover. After a failed
suicide attempt, she is left alone, desolate, but a grown-up
woman.

It is Lee's handling of the specifically science fictional
elements in this romance that not only subverts the
'message' of the plot as described above but also, I think,
challenges the male-dominated tradition within science
fiction of man (that is, man) and machine.

The Silver Metal Lover is set in a future world of depleted
population and a society split between the very rich and
the very poor. Technology can work wonders and is used
by Jane's mother Demeter to keep 'just so' everything
around her: a house up in the clouds programmed to
respond to her every wish, and a daughter in the house
whom she controls likewise, with capsules that determine
her weight and size and molecular restructuring for her
hair colour. But no-one, not even Demeter, can provide
what Jane really wants: the love of a good man. In this
world no such thing exists. Of Jane's male friends the
cynical, sybaritic Clovis is M-B, Mirror-Bias, while the
sinister Jason is too entwined with his twin sister Medea in
games of manipulation and violence to fulfil such a role.
The older men are all preserved with Rejuvinex. So Jane
falls in love with a robot, and not just any old robot like the
ones her mother has about the house. Her choice is a
Silver Ionised Locomotive Electronic robot, one of the
'Sophisticated Format' range from Electronic Metals Ltd,
that includes gold and copper versions too, each one with a
particular skill (S.I.L.V.E.R.'s being musical) as well as the
standard programme to please. It is left to Clovis to point
out to Jane the implications of a 'Sophisticated Format';
her actress friend Egyptia has recognised them immediately and has rushed S.I.L.V.E.R.'s into her bed, telling

Jane afterwards, 'It's ruined me for a man for weeks'. Jane yearns for love and understanding, and struggles against her lust: 'How could I ever hope to have a proper relationship with a man if I began by going to bed with a robot?' But, with a pleasurable predictability, lust and love will be combined as Silver slowly becomes a real man.

In science fictional terms robots are an old favourite. They are direct descendants of the hapless monster created by Mary Shelley's Dr Frankenstein. Like Frankenstein's monster, S.I.L.V.E.R. is unnamed; like the monster too he is made up of bits and pieces, not of other bodies but of electronic gadgetry. Jane buys the sum of the component parts; 'humanness' is not a part of the transaction. S.I.L.V.E.R. represents something 'other' than the real, but it is not the monstrous 'other' of Mary Shelley's *Frankenstein*. For where the latter can be read, like her *The Last Man*, as a fantasy 'of absolute negation or dissolution of cultural order',[21] with Frankenstein's desire for the 'other' leading to entropy and dissolution, Lee's tale is much more firmly within the romantic tradition. Transcendent solutions are offered; desire for the 'other' leads out of the self (losing oneself in love) rather than into the darkness within.

But *The Silver Metal Lover* refers back to *Frankenstein* not least because of the plethora of science fiction stories that have come between. While I would not claim that its subversive qualities are equal to those of Frankenstein, it is, I think, subversive of the monster robot trope of 20th century science fiction. Monsters, aliens and artificial intelligences are constructed as 'other', as repositories of fear and desire. But they are vanquished, for in pulp science fiction order is restored, entropy is kept at bay. Within monster stories women have a specific role: they provide the excuse for vanquishing the monster, for they inflame it with lust, and, as in *King Kong* for example, at the same time humanise it. In such stories women are at once available and forbidden; the lust they arouse is fearful in its power and must be contained. It is perhaps because sexual relationships were taboo in science fiction until the 1960s that there were so many aliens lusting for human females. It is not just monsters, robots and aliens that are constructed as 'other'; women, too, as mentioned earlier, fill that role. And there are the woman-as-robot stories in which they are not, indeed, unpredictable and terrifying monsters, but rather tame servants. This is woman stripped of autonomy and humanity, woman constructed to serve men.[22]

Often, then, the monsters of science fiction are destroyed or tamed; their subversive potential is recuperated and the status quo is further strengthened. Much the same fate awaits the fearsome m/other. But in the hands of women writers, robots and their cousins the androids and cyborgs can become quite a different kettle of metal. The playful and provocative Joanna Russ (perhaps the best known woman writer of science fiction after Ursula LeGuin) gives us the beautiful and useful Davy in *The Female Man*.[23] 'The original germ-plasm was chimpanzee ... but none of the behaviour is organically controlled any more').[24] Davy is guaranteed to shock any male reader who dares to think of himself as a 'feminist man' and indeed, some of the personae of Russ's multi-personae heroine. After a particularly satisfying bout with her monster-pet, Jael remarks laconically: 'Alas! those who were shocked at my making love that way to a man are now shocked at my making love to a machine; you can't win'.[25]

Joanna Russ is here playing with the unquestioned conventions of a genre: both the peripheral role of women and the use of robots as servitors are part of the tradition of pulp science fiction that she exploits to provocative effect. So too with Tanith Lee and her Silver Metal Lover. This robot is the stuff of any girl's dreams. He has burgundy hair and auburn eyes, mulberry boots and a black-red velvet cloak, a silver skin and a programme to please. He is a poet and a minstrel. He is clever, gentle and practical. When Jane leaves her mother's luxury house and rents a bare room in the slum area of town, Silver reads up on DIY and turns it almost overnight into a magical frescoed haven. Were they – impossibly – to have babies, Silver would undoubtedly take on his share of the childcare with pleasure. This is the new man, the man of the future. But it's not enough for Jane; following the conventions of romance she must make her hero love her, she must make him feel. Silver is at first resistant: 'You have a beautiful touch', he says when she is brushing his hair. 'So do you'. 'Mine is programmed'. But not even a robot can remain immune to the love of a good woman.

Silver's development from robot to human begins in small ways: his body feels warm rather than metal-cool, he admits to liking the taste of food, where before he had pretended. And as he becomes unprogrammed, so does Jane. Together they wander the town, busking for the rent money, and as Jane stops taking the pills that her mother had ordered, pills that were meant to make her voluptuous but only made her fat, and as her hair grows out of its molecular restructuring, she grows to look more and more like Silver. From ugly duckling to swanhood, from daughter to lover, from Jane to Jain: our poor little rich girl has found happiness, and it shows. 'Jain with her blonde hair, her twenty two inch waist, her silver skin, her peacock jacket, her cloak of emerald green velvet, lined with violet satin.[26] Jane marvels at her own transformation, and best of all, it's all natural. This is love on the dole: not much to eat; clothes from jumble stalls or bargained for in the market.

The crisis of the story comes when Silver reaches full humanity in orgasm, something that he has always faked before, and Jane achieves adulthood in her ability to get pleasure from someone else's pleasure: 'I felt what happened to him, the silent, violent upheaval shaking itself through him. Earthquake of the flesh. I was the one who cried out, as if the orgasm were mine. But my body was only shaken with his pleasure and my pleasure in his pleasure. So I knew what he'd known before, the joy in my lover's joy.'[27]

From then on it's downhill all the way. While Jane and Silver are discovering the pain of loving each other, the dependency and vulnerability of needing each other, the forces of evil are gathering in the background. For, of course, a robot so humanised as Silver poses too much of a

threat, and it has been obvious from the start that these
gleaming lovers are star-crossed. There is, however, a twist
at the end: robot lovers prove not so easy to be rid of as
might have been imagined.

So what has Tanith Lee done with this science fiction
tale? She has challenged the traditional role of robots,
creating one that serves a woman rather than a man. As in
the past women have been peripheral to the story,
expendable, even, in male-created futures, in this instance
it is men who are expendable. And it is precisely this that
brings about the demise of S.I.L.V.E.R.: he is altogether
too much of a threat to half of humanity.

More importantly, it seems to me, Lee is offering an
ironic commentary on the genres from which she is
borrowing and, more boldly, she is doing what SF at its
best always tries to do, offering an oblique if not ironic
commentary on the conditions under which we live. In a
world of male privilege the difficulties inherent in sexual
and emotional relationships between women and men are
legion: it is this that underpins the fairy tale nature of *The
Silver Metal Lover*, for Jane creates her own object of desire
and then breathes life into him. It is romantic fiction that
makes the impossible possible, that gives us lovers forever
young and satisfying. The hyperbole of such stories is
exploited stylishly by Tanith Lee, with the idealisation of
her lovers' looks, with their power to make the earth move
around them, with their passion that threatens the status
quo. Lee is at once using and mocking the form: she makes
the impossible possible, but only in impossible terms, then
sets it in a detailed and credible science fictional world of
the future.

Perhaps surprisingly, science fiction is not the place to
look for visions of how women and men might live
together in the future. It is an area that is pretty much
avoided by women writers. Exceptionally, the daring
Joanna Russ deals with the love between a woman and a
man in *The Two of Them*;[28] the outcome is deeply
pessimistic. Others, such as Marge Piercy in *Woman on the
Edge of Time*[29] and Ursula LeGuin in *The Dispossessed*,[30]
have as background to their stories the idea that women

and men can live together in new, non-oppressive ways, but neither of those writers brings the full force of their imaginations (and both have powerful ones) to bear on such a relationship. Other feminist writers envision futures in which there are no men at all, and certainly not men that could be lovers of women.

Does this reflect a difficulty that women have in writing about heterosexual love in the real world? It is, indeed, only in the narrative conventions of romantic fiction that it is presented as unproblematic. And here, in science fiction, Lee has given us an unproblematic relationship too: a dream of grandiose power, of woman triumphant, of man made according to woman's desire. Jane is a latter-day Frankenstein who both loves and is loved by her monster lover.

Notes

[1] Tanith Lee, *The Silver Metal Lover*, Unicorn, 1986.

[2] Rosemary Jackson, *Fantasy: The Literature of Subversion*, Methuen 1981.

[3] *Ibid*, p.158.

[4] *Ibid*, p.155.

[5] See Brian Aldiss, *Billion Year Spree*, Weidenfeld and Nicolson, 1973.

[6] Joanna Russ, 'Speculations: The Subjunctivity of Science Fiction', *Extrapolation*, Vol 15, No 1, December 1973.

[7] Tanith Lee, *The Birthgrave*, Futura 1977.

[8] Tanith Lee, *The Storm Lord*, Futura 1977.

[9] Tanith Lee, *Cyrion*, DAW 1982. The shorter pieces, 'Cyrion in Wax' and 'A Lynx with Lions' are in *Dreams of Darkness and Light: The Great Short Fiction of Tanith Lee*.

[10] Tanith Lee, 'Sirriamnis', *Dreams of Darkness and Light*.

[11] 'Flat Earth' series: *Night's Master*, Hamlyn 1981; *Death's Master*, Hamlyn 1982; *Delusion's Master*, Arrow 1986; *Delirium's Mistress*, Arrow 1987.

[12] Joanna Russ, 'The Clichès from Outer Space', in Green and Lefanu (eds), *Despatches from the Frontiers of the Female Mind*, The Women's Press 1985.

[13] Jessica Amanda Salmonson (ed), *Amazons!*, DAW 1979, p.14.

[14] Susan Wood, 'Women and Science Fiction', *Algol*, Winter 78/79.

[15] Marion Zimmer Bradley, *The Ruins of Isis*, Arrow 1980.

[16] Gerd Brandenberg, *The Daughters of Egalia*, Journeyman 1985.

[17] Tanith Lee, 'Northern Chess' in Salmonson, *op cit*.

[18] *Ibid*, p.175.

[19] Tanith Lee, *East of Midnight*, Macmillan 1977.
[20] Tanith Lee, *Don't Bite the Sun*, and *Drinking Sapphire Wine*, both published by Hamlyn in 1979.
[21] Jackson, *op cit*, p.99.
[22] There is sometimes an uneasiness in these stories, as if the narrative cannot quite contain the constructed 'other'. See, for example, Susan Wood's discussion of Lester Del Rey's notorious short story 'Helen O'Loy', in Wood, *op cit*.
[23] Joanna Russ, *The Female Man*, The Women's Press 1985.
[24] *Ibid*, p.199.
[25] *Ibid*, p.200.
[26] *Silver Metal Lover*, p.165.
[27] *Ibid*, p.164.
[28] Joanna Russ, *The Two of Them*, The Women's Press 1986.
[29] Marge Piercy, *Woman on the Edge of Time*, The Women's Press, 1979.
[30] Ursula LeGuin, *The Dispossessed*, Gollancz 1974.

Fictional Fathers

JON COOK

Chamber of Horrors

Freud thought emotional ambivalence towards the father was the basis of civilisation. To explain this he told a horror story about origins. Like Darwin, Freud thought the first form of human society was the primal horde dominated by the strongest male, the father, who denied his sons sexual access to the females in the group. Our first father, 'violent and jealous' as Freud describes him, drove the sons out of the horde as they grew up. No doubt they spent some time sulking on the sidelines, but one day the sons realised the potential of fraternal conspiracy and banded together to murder the father. They then devoured him to show that they were all in it together and, more importantly, to accomplish an unconscious aim: the internalisation of the father's strength, which they both envied and feared. But the first feast was followed by the first hangover. Once they had rid themselves of the monster, the brothers realised how much they loved him. To assuage their guilt and remorse, they created the first sign, a totem, the father substitute. Around the totem, the father's power was recreated in the form of taboo, the two primary laws against incest and murder. The brothers deposed the tyrant only to renew his law. Out of their complicity in the common crime emerged the social form described by Freud as the 'fraternal clan'.

The totem is the first fictional father and it is born out of the murder of a real father. The psychic functions of this fictional father are complex and contradictory in their relation to the murderous brothers. By recreating the father in the totem, the brothers can pretend that they haven't done what they have done at the same time as they commemorate the act: the totem both replaces the father and marks the fact of his murder. But the totem is also an opportunity to create a 'good' fantasy father in place of the 'bad' real one:

> The totemic system was, as it were, a covenant with their father, in which he promised them everything that a childish imagination may expect from a father ... while on their side they undertook to respect his life, that is to say, not to repeat the deed which had brought destruction on their real father. Totemism, moreover, contained an attempt at self-justification: 'If our father had treated us in the way the totem does, we should never have felt tempted to kill him.' In this fashion totemism helped to smooth things over and to make it possible to forget the event to which it owed its origin.[1]

Forgetting may have been helped by the aniconic nature of the totem. The father is recreated not in his own image but in the form of an animal or some other creature or event in the natural world. The emergence of a god in human form was, according to Freud, a momentous event in the evolution of human culture. It marked a renewed longing for the father, a further twist in the basic pattern of emotional ambivalence towards him: hatred and veneration, revulsion and yearning, each feeling intertwined with its apparent opposite, and finding expression through it. The father god appears once the bitterness and aggression that produced the first parricide has waned. The new image reflects a fundamental change in social life, the reinstatement of the father, not as the violent leader of the primal horde but as the benign head of a family organised around the twin taboos on incest and murder. The trace of the primal horde remains within the patriarchal family, the form of its unconscious life, but it has been civilised by what Freud calls 'the social achievements of the fraternal clan'. We know these included the creation of totem and taboo, but the brothers also agreed upon a moral bond: none of them would do to the other what they had all done collectively to their father. The prohibition acknowledges and seeks to suppress the desire within each of the brothers to kill his fellows and take the place of the murdered father.

And so the story goes on, always the same but different. In *Moses and Monotheism*, Freud recasts the history of Judaism and Christianity according to the motif of the murdered father. He does this by reading out of the Bible a hidden history which has been deliberately disguised in the composition of the Mosaic text. Hence, the original sin was not eating the apple but parricide. The apparent continuity of the Judaic tradition, invented in the 'priestly narrative', masks a gap between Moses and the late Jewish religion, a gap caused by the murder of Moses by the Jews as they rejected the austere religion, without ceremony or magic, that he tried to impose upon them. In the murder of Moses, the jews re-enact the first parricide, and, like their predecessors, are compelled to both expiate their crime and forget it. Christ is incorporated into the narrative in order to enact a fantasy of atonement for the original sin. But within the figure of Christ other traces can be discerned: not just the meek redeemer, but the hero who rebelled against the harsh law of the father, the ring-leader of the fraternal clan. Ambivalence towards the father is worked through in the 'new' religion of Christianity, just as it had been in the older 'primitive' religions of totem and taboo:

> Ostensibly aimed at propitiating the father god, it ended in his being dethroned and got rid of. Judaism has been a religion of the father; Christianity became a religion of the son. The old God the Father fell back behind Christ; Christ, the Son, took his place just as every son had hoped to do in primaeval times.[2]

At the very moment when guilt towards the father is assuaged in the sacrifice of the son, the lineaments re-emerge of what caused the guilt in the first place, rebellion against the father. In *Totem and Taboo* and *Moses and Monotheism* Freud shows how religions are the product of a violent ambivalence towards the father. In both texts he draws out the analogy between the development of religions and the form of the human psyche. The history that was once played out in the primal horde, that recurred in the murder of Moses and the Crucifixion, occurs yet again in the unconscious life of the child. The same murderous fantasy directed towards the father followed by the same guilt and remorse; the same desire to be rid of the father and to be the father. The mind becomes a chamber of horrors presided over by a dark patriarchal image.

In 1819 the Spanish painter, Goya, bought a house near Madrid. Old and profoundly deaf, he called his new home the *Quinta del Sordo*, the deaf man's house. On its walls he painted a series of frescoes, sometimes called 'the black paintings'. One of these, perhaps the most famous, is of Saturn devouring his children.[3]

Goya was not the first painter to treat this mythical subject. The myth itself dates back at least to classical antiquity. The story it tells is, in a sense, without date or origin: Saturn or Chronus married his sister Rhea, but their marriage is burdened by a prophecy that one of Saturn's sons will dethrone him. To prevent the fulfilment of the prophesy, Saturn eats the children born to him by Rhea, until she manages to smuggle away her third son, Zeus, who in due course deposes his father. The scene of Saturn devouring his children was not depicted in antiquity. It stayed off-stage, unrepresented. But in the 14th century, the scene finds its way into the title vignettes of books and illustrations for them. There is, of course, an allegorical motivation: Saturn is Chronus; Chronus is Time; Time devours its Children. The coolness of allegory surrounds the violence of the scene. In one picture Saturn sinks his teeth into the child's arm, in another he has devoured its head. In one remarkable drawing, from the early 15th century, as Saturn devours one child, another castrates him. But again the scene is depicted in a detached way. Bodies do not writhe

in pain. The child is eaten, the father is castrated, as
though these were everyday events. The anonymous artist
may well have conflated two different episodes of the
mythic story into one scene. Before he was overthrown by
Zeus, Saturn had himself overthrown his father, Uranus,
and, as the mark of his triumph, had castrated him. The
effect of the conflation is to bring together two
contradictory fantasies: dreams of being eaten by the
father are, according to Freud, representations of the
anxiety of being castrated by him. What we have in the
picture is a simultaneous representation of that anxiety
and its opposite: the castrator castrated.[4]

Goya's depiction of the myth is radically different from
earlier treatments of it. The coolness of allegory has
disappeared. We are confronted with the horror head on.
The earlier pictures had shown Saturn in profile. Here
Saturn stares at us out of the dark background in the
picture. He has none of the signs of kingship or deity that
were customary in the portrayal of Saturn – no wreaths,
crowns or sickles. He is a demented, naked giant who
clutches the half-eaten body of his child in front of him. It
is as though we have caught him in the act. Allegory has
been replaced by nightmare, an effect that is heightened
by Saturn's indeterminate shape. He comes out of
blackness and merges back into it.

What is the picture saying? Perhaps it's just a monstrous
joke: Goya had the picture in his dining room, part of the
chamber of horrors which he made out of the 'House of
the Deaf Man'. Where Goya ate his meals, Saturn
devoured his children. Confronted with the picture or
with similar examples of Goya's art, some commentators
start to mumble in embarrassment: 'obsessive fantasies',
'troubled mind', 'morbid imagination', 'old age', 'political
disillusionment'. The picture is a symptom of the artist's
diseased state, and it does not speak to us about anything
more than that. But, of course, Goya did not invent the
subject. The myth preceded him, however original his
treatment of it. But this myth tends to stay on the margins
of representation, even when it is represented at all, in the
form of book illustrations at a time when books had a very

limited circulation or, in the case of Goya's picture, as a painting on the wall of a private house, only later transferred, after the artist's death, to the public space of the gallery. The culture here finds an embarrassing reflection, one that it does not want to be reminded of too often: not just Goya's disease alone, but something more pervasive. Saturn eats his children. Time devours what time creates. The problem with the allegorical reading is that it fails to capture the perversion of natural process represented by the scene. Saturn, the fictional father, eats his children. He denies birth, putting into his mouth what the mother produced from her womb. He denies birth because he knows from the prophecy that it threatens his craving for absolute dominion. Goya's picture reveals this as madness, the madness of the father, of the tyrant who wants to stop the fact of change and succession because change and succession will bring an end to his power.

Freud invents a story about sons devouring their father and thinks this explains why civilisation exists: '... the beginnings of religion, morals, society and art converge in the Oedipus complex.'[5] In the story of Saturn, a father devours his children. In the Freudian scheme the two stories would be one: Saturn is an imaginary reconstruction of the father in the primal horde, threatening death to whoever challenges him, or, more specifically, theatening castration to any of the sons who threaten his sexual monopoly. He is the product of a culture grown guilty and anxious about its challenge to paternal power, a nightmare dreamt by the brothers after they have murdered their father. He is the father born from intense fear, the structural opposite, in terms of the pattern of ambivalence, to the father as an object of adoration.

But there are other patterns and preoccupations running through these narratives and pictures. To imagine the father is almost at once to imagine a history of violence. The father is placed as both originator and victim of the violence that surrounds him. His stories centre on tyrannical power and its overthrow, on murder, rebellion, sacrifice, cannibalism and castration. The emotional constellation appropriate to these stories contains hatred, jealousy, sadistic domination, masochistic submission, and always a structure of feeling characterised by duplicity: love disguised as hate, and vice versa. There are, too, certain modes of perception modelled on the relation to the father, notably paranoia:

> ... The model upon which paranoiacs base their delusions of persecution is the relation of a child to his father. A son's picture of his father is habitually clothed with excessive powers of this kind, and it is found that distrust of the father is intimately linked with admiration for him. When a paranoiac turns the figure of one of his associates into a 'persecutor', he is raising him to the rank of a father: he is putting him into a position in which he can blame him for all his misfortunes.[6]

And, of course, it is a part of this paranoid system that power is invested in the father, or his stand-in, not as a matter of the rational delegation of duties and responsibilities but as 'mana', a kind of magical emanation. Power cannot be separated from the person of the father. It is there in him, beyond all reason. The irrational character of the father's power is such that it survives his death. One meaning of Freud's story in *Totem and Taboo* is that the murder of the father brings him to life. Rather than dissolving his power, death magnifies and perpetuates it. His death in nature produces his life in culture as symbol (a totem or a god), as source of the law, and as the subject of a seemingly unresolvable ambivalence, oscillating between hatred and veneration, identification with the father and rejection of him. There is a Gothic feel to this. The murdered father becomes the prototype of the undead, reaching out from the grave to control and terrify the living. We can discern his trace in Dracula, or, indeed, in that whole apparatus of 19th century fiction which represents character as constrained by the will of some dead father figure.[7]

The irrationality appears to derive from the denial of some primary 'sense-making' distinction, as between the living and the dead, or, in Saturn's case, as between what

you can eat and what you can't. But there is a logic of sorts
at work in these transgressions and one that is closely
connected to the father's birth-in-death. What this permits
is a doubling or splitting of the image of the father, or,
more properly, the father's image is created in this
doubling. One example of this can be found in Freud's
analysis of the sacrificial scene in *Totem and Taboo*. He
argues that in the sacrificial ritual the father 'is in fact
represented twice over – as the god and as the totemic
animal'. This double representation creates a structure in
which the sacrifice can be both to the god and of the god
(the analogy with the Crucifixion is evident):

> The two-fold presence of the father corresponds to the two
> chronologically successive meanings of the scene. The
> ambivalent attitude towards the father has found a plastic
> expression in it, and so, too, has the victory of the son's
> affectionate emotions over his hostile ones. *The scene of the
> father's vanquishment, of his greatest defeat, has become the stuff for
> the representation of his greatest triumph.* The importance which
> is everywhere, without exception, ascribed to sacrifice lies in
> the fact that it offers satisfaction to the father for the outrage
> inflicted on him in the same act in which the deed is
> commemorated. (my emphasis)[8]

The sacrificial scene is marked by paradox. It represents
two contradictory statements as both true: the father
triumphs and the father is defeated. The 'plastic
expression' of the paradox can occur because the father's
image is doubled, as triumphant god and vanquished
animal. Despite Freud's suggestion that the two meanings
of the scene are chronologically successive, that the ritual
action of sacrifice holds the two terms of the paradox
apart, his own formulation of the statement made by that
action is itself paradoxical.

According to recent work done in communication
theory, notably by Anthony Wilden, paradox is at the
heart of that communicative knot called the double-bind.[9]
Double-binds abound in communication: the injunction,
'do not read this', would be one example, where the
recipient of the message can neither obey or disobey it. If

the message is to be obeyed, it cannot be read; if it is not read, it cannot be a message; if it is read, the message is disobeyed, and so on. It may not be that double-bound messages of this kind are uniquely the property of the father or his derivatives, but they are nonetheless closely associated with him in psychoanalytic theory. This is not simply to do with the long established connection between fathers and imperatives, although double-binds are always at some level to do with the issuing of unstated commands. The Oedipal situation, which we can for the moment read in terms of the father-mother-son triangle, dictates a paradoxical injunction from father to son: 'do not be me because I do what you must not do to your mother' paraphrases one half of the paradox, and 'be me, a man with a wife of his own' gives the other. In relation to the daughter, the father's presence in the Oedipal triangle multiplies the number of double-binds. The following would just be a start:

1. 'Do not be a daughter, but a son. Be what you are not and cannot be.'
2. 'Be like your mother, let me seduce you'/'Do not be like your mother, do not let me seduce you, preserve my law'.
3. 'Do not be like your mother, let me seduce you'/'Be like your mother, prevent me from seducing you'.

These are rough paraphrases of the opening gambits in the conversation of the unconscious. No doubt, further examples could be given on the side of the son or the daughter, but my proposal is that what they would have in common is the character of paradoxical injunction, the double-bind. It is, of course, important to stress that the examples are *paraphrases*. What is paraphrased are the messages carried in the medium of the unconscious, and therefore subject to its typical laws of revision and repression into scenes of dream and fantasy, ritual and fiction, or the overwhelming unsaid of everyday life. Within this medium, the father is surrounded by an aura of paradoxical injunction. Desire is regulated in the name of the father, but according to the logic of the double-bind. The father at once invites and denies the desire of others, but in doing so, he is left with the problem of his own desire. Here we come across another paradox, whether the author of a law is subject to his own law, or, more specifically, whether the father is constrained by the law against incest, which is authorised in his name.

If the father regulates desire, he also dictates identity, or tries to do so: 'be a son, be this kind of son', 'be a daughter, be this kind of daughter', and so on. But, of course, this dictation does not go unopposed, given the rivalrous and strife-torn nature of Freud's narratives about culture and family life. The father occupies a strategic place in what Wilden has called 'a Hegelian struggle for recognition'. This refers us to the *Phenomenology of Mind* where Hegel develops an argument about the crucial dependence of self-consciousness upon recognition: 'Self-consciousness attains its satisfaction only in another self-consciousness.'[10] This satisfaction consists in knowing ourselves in another, that is in knowing that another recognises us. But, for Hegel, self-consciousness is a form of desire, an energy which is constantly seeking to identify itself in others. In his analysis of Hegel's *Phenomenology*. Jean Hyppolite has written about this relation of desire and recognition:

> ... the desire of life becomes the desire of another desire, or rather, in view of the necessary reciprocity of the phenomenon, human desire is always *desire of the desire of another*. Thus, in human love, desire appears to the self as the desire of the desire of another. The self needs to be beheld by the other. For the self is essentially desire. Thus what the self expects to find in the Other is desire of its desire.[11]

This gives a blissful account of the dialectics of desire and recognition which, as Hegel and Hyppolite knew, was complicated by the facts of domination and struggle. The mutuality of recognition, which is one of the desired goals of self-consciousness, cannot occur in the face of social inequality. Hegel tells this story in his famous didactic of master and slave, where the master demands a recognition from the slave which he in turn is not prepared to give. This, as it turns out, is not all to the disadvantage of the slave, whose relationship to the material world through labour enables him to develop in a way that the master, the simple consumer of that labour, cannot. The master is caught in what Hegel elsewhere calls 'the motionless tautology' of a self-consciousness which is cut off from recognition by another person and from development through work in the material world.[12]

Hegel's master bears some resemblance to the father of the double-bind. There is an important difference, too: the power of the master is surpassed by the dialectical process, whereas the father's authority is preserved by the double-bind. But what both have in common is a refusal of recognition. Like Hegel's master, the father is a figure who requires recognition of himself, while refusing it to others. In terms of the Oedipal triangle, the father requires the son to recognise his desire in what the father wishes, at the same time as he refuses to recognise the son's desire as independent from his own. With the daughter, the father requires her to recognise his own desire, to feel responsible for it, but refuses to recognise her own – which may well be, in these depressed circumstances, little more than the desire to say no.

Various kinds of cultural evidence group around this thesis about the father and recognition. One example is the recurrent phenomenon in religion of a taboo against naming or figuring the father god – and, in this context, naming and figuring are ways of making the father recognisable. The power of this taboo is culturally variable, and, as with most taboos, there are ways around it. The father god can be figured indirectly, in disguise. But the token sign recreates the awesome power rather than making it knowable. Behind the represented god stands another, whose mystery is so great that it can never be named or known. Behind the manifest power, there is a higher inscrutable power. The father god always stands at the very limit of representation, caught in its terms only on sufferance.

King Lear is not a god, although he has the pretensions

to be one. He walks on stage and sets his daughter an impossible test. The test is about their recognition of him: which of them loves him most. No doubt, the old man is anxious about the men that two of his daughters are hanging out with: the paternal order is punctuated by a rivalry without end. Goneril and Regan take up the challenge with enthusiasm. They know that there are rich pickings to be made out of Lear's stupidity. Cordelia registers her protest by the formality of her response. But there is one rule that binds all the daughters. They cannot turn the tables on their father. They cannot ask him which of them he loves most. Lear is not required to recognise them, and, indeed, the whole dynamic of the play is about the cost and the question of bringing the father to recognition. Whether the father is ever brought to recognition is something the play leaves open. Lear finds the answer to his questions. Cordelia loves him most, but, knowing that, he then wraps her in a beautiful incestuous fantasy, an imprisoned world where only he and she will live. Her death ruins that fantasy but leaves their relationship in paradox: Lear recognises his daughter in her death, but cannot bear to sustain that recognition in his own life.

Or, as another bit of cultural evidence, we can return to the picture, *Saturn Devouring his Children*. Goya paints Saturn caught in the act. He stares at us out of the picture – stares at us, but does not see us. If he acknowledged the spectator, he would have to recognise what he is doing, or acknowledge our recognition of what he is doing. But that is impossible. Goya paints a father god gone mad in his own *defence*. In order to do what he does, he cannot recognise what he is doing. The absence of recognition is a condition of the violence, of the violent death that the painting depicts. In *Saturn Devouring his Children*, Goya returns to a subject that he had depicted in the engravings entitled the *Disasters of War* and in his famous painting, *The Third of May, 1808*. It is as though he saw violent death as the central emblem of his own time and culture, and violent death is always for Goya represented by a drama of non-recognition. In *The Third of May, 1808* the victim of the firing squad looks to his executioners. But they do not look back at him. Their heads are bent over their rifles. Their faces are invisible to the spectator.[13] In *Saturn Devouring His Children* we see the face of the murderer turned to us. But the face is without recognition. The effect is to compound rather than mitigate the horror. In the picture of Saturn, Goya disclosed the archaic origin of what he observed in his own time; he finds it in a mythic father.

There is an obvious, recurrent association of the father with death: in Goya; in Hegel, where death is the Absolute Master; in Freud, where the murder of the father is the first 'cultural' death, the first death to be symbolised; and, for good measure, the association can be found in Lacan's writing, where 'the Law, the symbolic father, insofar as he signifies that Law, is actually the dead father'.[14] Lacan reminds us of the third term in the paternal set: not just the association with death, but through that association, the father signifies the Law, as its author. We are back with the father as the archetype of the living dead, and with the paradox that the Law is the act of the dead. But it is just as much to the point that the Law is repeatedly associated with violence. The violence can be done to the father or by the father. What is represented in one and the same paternal story is the violence that begets the Law, that makes it necessary, and the violence within the Law, the violence that, in the end, makes it effective. But within this story there is another one, as we have seen: the father is the author of the Law, but, as its author, he has the privilege of being outside it. The father is not just, as Lacan would have it, the signifier of the Law. He signifies its opposite, too, a power unconstrained by any rule.

'... try to think of your father'

Of course, we know all this stuff about fathers, these Freudian myths and their Lacanian elaborations. The story is a stale one, out-of-date. After all, if Freud and his followers try to reinstate the power of the father in our unconscious minds, that is exactly because the father was losing his authority in the real world. The castration complex is a rear-guard action. In attempting to re-empower the father, psychoanalysis fulfils its own secret aim – to create a mystique of masculine power around the figure of the analyst, so that we want him even when we no longer need him, just like father. Outside this closed world things are different. The real story is about the steady erosion of paternal authority. Economic development has long since done away with the practical power of the father to regulate what is produced and to pass on the skills necessary for production. The anonymous order of multinational corporations has replaced the intimate tyranny of the family firm. Fathers are old hat. They have nothing to give. Their modern representative is not Lear or Saturn or the God of *Paradise Lost*, but someone like the heroine's father in Dickens's novel, *Little Dorrit*, all fluttering fingers and fuss, jealous, paranoid, his only power an elaborate fiction sustained by the pity and love of those around him, a fiction whose purpose is to protect him against the knowledge of his failure. William Dorrit, like all fathers, had to be deceived. We know that from the story of Saturn and his children, or from Goneril and Regan's glozing of the old man in *King Lear*. But *Little Dorrit* marks a shift in the motive for deception. The lie is necessary not because the father is to be feared, nor because there's something to be wheedled out of him, but because he has to be protected from knowing the truth of his condition.

The history of 19th and 20th century western culture abounds with texts like *Little Dorrit*. While these texts register the psychic damage inflicted by paternal power, they also show it being hollowed out from within, or develop tactics for a successful resistance or escape. Subject to scepticism, fathers appear to move to the margins of the text, where they occupy positions of sentiment, nostalgia, or barren rationality. They are the epitomes of delusion, pious, drunken wrecks, like Simon Dedalus in Joyce's *Ulysses*.

One hypothesis would be that this shift does not simply register a loss in the economic status of fathers, but a change in the nature and distribution of power itself. This, at least, would be a corollary of the distinction Michel Foucault proposes between ancient and modern power. According to Foucault, ancient power depended upon the idea of a public space, and of an authority which manifested itself in this space in the figure of the sovereign. The sovereign embodied the law and made it visible. His power was concerned with orders and obedience, with what Foucault has described as 'the right to decide life and death'. In this context, political theory was concerned with resolving questions about the nature and the limits of this sovereign power. By constrast, modern power operates by techniques of surveillance. It is concerned to establish behavioural norms, to create new kinds of subject, new forms of desire. It is anonymous, without any visible sovereign as its locus and centre. The father's decline, then, can be mapped on to the shift from ancient to modern power, given that the father was the typical form of the sovereign. As modern power takes over from the old, so the political, economic, legal and cultural links which connected the father to power are undone – hence William Dorrit, Simon Dedalus, and the rest. The old man becomes a shadow of his former self, all washed up and nowhere to go.[15]

Or so the argument goes. Yet there are grounds for thinking that what this shift in representation indicates is not a simple erosion of paternal power. If the modern period has seen a decline in the functional authority of the father – his power to command in politics, economy, and the law – it has also seen a recreation of that power in a bizarre theatre of desire which finds its most evident locus in the family, but extends beyond that to suffuse the seemingly anonymous character of modern power with the characteristic sounds of the bartering of male privilege. In Dickens' novel, William Dorrit may have lost all his money, but this does not subdue his authority over his daughter, although its basis is in her desire to please him and, indeed, whoever replaces him. His pathos becomes his privilege.

Again, Foucault's writings supply a historical context for

understanding this change in the power of the father. In the first volume of *The History of Sexuality*, Foucault distinguishes between two different forms of sexual relation, 'the deployment of alliance' and 'the deployment of sexuality'. The first of these is traditional, persistent and widespread:

> … a system of marriage, of fixation and development of kinship ties, of transmission of names and possessions.[16]

As anthropological evidence has shown, this system need not be tied to paternal authority, although in western culture it has typically been so.

The deployment of sexuality is modern, volatile, and distinctive of western cultures. It takes shape from the 18th century onwards, in marked contrast with the deployment of alliance:

> The deployment of alliance is built around a system of rules defining the permitted and the forbidden, the licit and the illicit, whereas the deployment of sexuality operates according to mobile, polymorphous and contingent techniques of power. The deployment of alliance has as one of its chief objectives to reproduce the interplay of relations and maintain the law that governs them; the deployment of sexuality, on the other hand, engenders a continual extension of areas and forms of control. For the first, what is pertinent is the link between partners and definite statutes; the second is concerned with the sensations of the body, the quality of pleasures, and the nature of impressions, however tenuous or imperceptible these may be. Lastly, if the deployment of alliance is firmly tied to the economy due to the role it can play in the transmission or circulation of wealth, the deployment of sexuality is linked to the economy through numerous and subtle relays, the main one of which, however, is the body – the body that produces and consumes.[17]

Although Foucault develops the differences between the two deployments in a terminology of contrast, they are by no means mutually exclusive. One important site of their interaction is the family, and the preoccupation of psychoanalysis with the family provides both an example and an episode of the relations between 'sexuality' and 'alliance'. At first, according to Foucault, psychoanalysis appears to threaten the family as a system of alliance, not least by taking the individual away from the control of the family, the better to discern the workings of a sexuality which seemed to undermine the pieties of family life. But this apparent move against the family was in fact part of a larger strategy which defined sexuality in terms of the system of familial alliance itself. Sexuality was not constituted outside the law, but in its terms. Psychoanalysis preached a reassuring message to the family because it was through the 'Object Mother' or 'the sovereign sign' of the Father that we gained access to our desire. At a moment when the economic and juridicial power was draining away from the deployment of alliance in the family, when father's firm had gone bankrupt or the means test was being applied or death duties levied, psychoanalysis produced a definition of sexuality which, according to Foucault, 'gave body and life to the rules of alliance by saturating them with desire'.[18] One implication of this new 'body and life' was to place the power of the father within the individual psyche. The authority which had tradition-ally been exercised from without, in a series of prohibitions, constraints, diktats, in a formal almost law-like discourse, was now reproduced in the work of the unconscious, in the whispering language of erotic obligation: not simply to obey your father, but to think of him, have him on your mind and in your mind in order to work out who you are.

All this was not just the arbitrary invention of psychoanalysis. Psychoanalysis restates, with the seeming authority of a scientific language, motifs that had been at work for years in 19th century narrative. Amy Dorrit is not the only 19th century heroine with her father on her mind. It is part of the necessary credentials of the heroine that she has a special relation with her father or to some figure of paternal authority. The matter is subject to endless variation. Little Dorrit mothers her father and then mothers her lover too, as though her fate was to move submissively on from William Dorrit to Arthur Clennam, two different characters who nonetheless occupy an equivalent place in the heroine's emotional life, as though father love was the only form of love permitted to her; Maggie Tulliver, in George Eliot's *The Mill on the Floss*, loves her father with a passion, feels the privilege of that love, and then dies by drowning, locked in her brother's embrace, as though her only real desires were incestuous; Emma's father, in Jane Austen's novel, is a feeble, querulous, old buffer. We are invited to feel that his weakness has permitted his daughter's moral giddiness. Her fate is to be educated by the dark, paternal authority of Mr Knightley and then to be safely locked up by him in marriage. A powerful masculinity replaces a weak one in her life, but they are both versions of the same authority which she must learn to love. The fictional father plays a central part in this pattern of relations, given that a fictional father is not simply a character in a novel who happens to be a father, but the paradigm of desirable masculinity itself; not simply what stories are about but the motive for telling them in the first place.

A parallel sexual script, centred on the fictional father, is at work in contemporary popular romances. The heroine of popular romance falls in love with the man of her dreams, but the man of her dreams turns out to be an emblem of patriarchal authority itself. Just in case there was any question about it, the romantic hero of a Mills and Boon novel seals off any doubts about the power of a masculine identity modelled upon the symbolism of the father. All the familiar ingredients are there: the threat of violence, the law-giving nature, the ownership of the world, a power vested in physical presence. Here comes Joss Varney – notice that poetry of the virile name – in *Devils Gold* by Nicola West:

> ... He moved as if he owned the entire airport, and even in the rough blue denims that he wore, she could see that his body must be as hard and fit as an athlete's, his broad shoulders stretching the faded shirt, his legs long and lean in the close fitting jeans.[19]

Modern romance contains many such specular moments, when the heroine gazes at the hero's physique. Jarret Earle – that virile name again, – is the hero of Margery Hilton's *Snow Bride*. He looks like this:

> He was tall, over six feet she estimated, broad of shoulder and slim of hip in the elegantly waisted grey suit. She got the impression that his mouth did not laugh easily, and there was hidden sensuousness in the long curve of the lower lip. His skin was lightly tanned, hinting at a fairly recent sojourn in a sunnier clime, his hair thick and dark, and his eyes the colour of lakeland slate with fringes of black lashes to contradict the coolness they framed.[20]

What is happening in these descriptions? Obviously there is a statement about physical attractiveness, desirability. Unlike its 19th century forbears, modern romance is not especially coy about sex. Bodies are undressed and observed, breasts and thighs are caressed. As our hero and heroine get closer to each other's genitals, the language becomes vaguer, but that vagueness is itself part of something more, a formulation of ecstacy:

> At last he was her beloved, taking her with him on a surging tide to the shores of ecstasy. Where there were no more doubts, no bitterness, only the supreme fulfilment of giving and taking of one another.[21]

This is the ultimate goal of the romantic heroine, hence the 'at last'. Her aim, although she may not know it to begin with, is to be possessed securely, to get those tall bodies and broad shoulders, those slim hips, and long, lean legs to take responsibility for her desire, 'taking her with him on a surging tide to the shores of ecstasy'. But getting to the shores of ecstasy is no easy task. The body of the romantic hero may represent an ideal of masculine beauty, but beauty here is the equivalent of physical strength, and physical strength itself becomes a sign of something more, a definition of authentic virility as a power that is always scarcely contained. (Joss Varney's

broad shoulders don't simply fit into his faded shirt, they
stretch it.) This power habitually threatens the romantic
heroine with the possibility of rape or some other form of
violence:

> He was moody and restless, with a betrayal of pent-up energy
> surging under a strict rein. She knew the mood well enough
> by now and sighed inwardly, preparing herself for the
> conflict that was about to come ...[22]

Sighing inwardly is very much to the point. It epitomises
the heroine's response to the threat of violence embodied
in the hero. It is part of her trial by ordeal. It may even
lead her to a momentary rejection of the hero but her love
for him always pulls her back into the game which will in
the end, momentarily, make him confess his love for her.
The rejection, the hostility, the anger can only be
temporary because the hero's violence is an aspect of his
strength, and it is that strength the heroine wants, because
the definition and purpose of her desire is to be possessed
by strength.

But romantic fiction does not simply offer a generalised
endorsement of masculine power. It discriminates
between forms of masculinity and the heroine learns this
discrimination – hence that other stereotype, the wimp:

> ... Stuart was pleasant and fun to be with. He'd been friendly
> from the first moment they'd met, the sort of person with
> whom she could feel completely at ease.[23]

The wimp is not unattractive. He offers the heroine a
break from vertiginous intensities of her attachment to
Joss, Jarrett, Rutt or whoever. He is often a 'womaniser',
and his presence induces relaxation rather than terror.
The prospect is sympathetic pleasure but the heroine
knows this is not enough. The wimp is not what the
romantic hero is. He is not an owner of mines,
corporations, airlines or other bits of the world. He cannot
see through the heroine to the true nature of her desire.
His fairness makes him bland and fraternal. He cannot

bring about in her that new condition of yearning which the hero authors and which makes all substitutes unacceptable.

Any fiction of this kind could be sub-titled how to take pleasure in being dominated. It offers a version of sexuality accordingly. But the sadism is not unconditional. When the heroine surrenders to her desire, we know that she desires to surrender, but she does so only on condition that the romantic hero confesses his love for her and agrees to marry. Ecstacy is premissed on a bargain: his love for her sex. The bargain is pleasurable on both sides. He finds pleasure in the confession of love because love is something he has learned to deny and fear, often as the result of a terrible experience in earlier life. She finds pleasure in the confession of sex because she can give freely to the hero what he has brought about in her and not fear the ruin of her identity. The formula of the bargain creates a kind of symmetry, a pretence of equality. The father of desire meets the mother of love and they exchange gifts. Each makes the other complete in a fantasy of total union.

But the bargain is also, on the heroine's part, about attaching desire to social convention, to propriety, to marriage. It is part of her traditional role that she should represent virtue. In modern romance that virtue is tried by the threat or temptation of sex outside marriage which is tantamount to the same thing as sex without love. Marriage is the guarantee of the hero's confession of love. If we translate this formula into Foucauldian terms, we could say that the romantic heroine brings the deployment of alliance, with its emphasis on kinship and constraint, into contact with the deployment of sexuality, with its emphasis on pleasure and sensation. Her function is to link the two, to reassure us that, in the end, desire and the law are compatible. But this can be a tricky business. The typical situation of the romantic heroine is to be in a state of transition between two men, her father and her husband. Or, it would be more accurate to say that the purpose of romantic narrative is to ensure this transition. At the beginning of a popular romance, the heroine is a kind of floating property. She may have a career. She may even have the temerity to think that a career is what she really wants. She may well have grown sceptical of romantic attachments to men. These formulae, and others, signal the fact that she is no longer directly contained within the family, the system of alliance. Or, as in *Snow Bride*, the family may be thrown into crisis by illness or financial catastrophe. What this means is that the power of men, and especially the father who regulates the system of alliance, has been temporarily suspended. The romantic hero comes into this situation as a hyper-patriarch who restores authority over the heroine. In *Snow Bride* this is done through a series of references to hands. They act as a code of the transition. The heroine's father 'had always held the controlling reins firmly in his own hands', but these hands weaken when he has a stroke. One of the first things the heroine notices about the hero is his 'well-shaped but strong hands' and, of course, it's not long before she is clinging to them, and then seeing their erotic potential, 'the hint of sensuousness in the long fingers that almost caressed the swelling curve of the coffee pot handle'. It is not spelled out in so many words, but the heroine is passed from the weakened grip of the father to the powerful, sexy hands of the hero. Her relationship to him is filial. He protects her against the world and herself. It is not surprising that he should remind her of her father:

> 'I suggest you put the matter out of your head for a few days. I'll let you know as soon as there's anything to report'.
> *And don't build up on getting it!* She read the warning unspoken between the lines. How often had her father said to Pippa or herself: 'Now don't build up on it lass' ...[24]

The basic pattern is repeated over and over again. Restoring masculine authority over the heroine is to induce dependence in her. Her resistance to physical violence becomes an adjunct to a larger display of power and another kind of bargain, not love for sex, but dependence for desire. Romantic fiction proposes a simple message: woman's desire depends upon dependence, as though the paradigm of desire was in a child's feeling for her parent, a daughter's for her father. But it is part of the extravagance and the ecstasy of this dependence that the romantic hero does not simply repeat and replace the heroine's father. He is the father writ large, masculine magnificence restored, and what that means in modern romance is that he is a capitalist, a creator of wealth and a master of commodities. As a result the heroine's agony and her ecstasy take place in well-padded cells. Here is one place where Con Brandon wooes the resisting heroine:

> ... Gala let out a little gasp. The rooms beyond were magnificent, furnished in a symphony of blues and greys. The tone was set by a massive autumnal painting of Lake Coniston that hung over the Adam-style fireplace, and picked up in the shimmering blue drapes at each arched window, the grey silk coverings on the Empire furniture, the misty carpeting ...[25]

This supercharged *Homes and Gardens* prose is a recurrent feature. Of course this is what every woman dreams of, especially if you are a heroine of modest means, and it is all the more exciting because it's his. The environment speaks of his power, his power to make her dreams real.

So the ecstasy is not just sexual, it's economic too. The sexual potency of the hero is at one with his economic potency. When Kelly Francis first meets Joss Varney in *Devil's Gold* she thinks him a vulgar roughneck, but that just shows what a silly little thing she is, as ex-fiancé, Mark, explains:

> Joss Varney's not just a gold dredger. He's my *boss* – my boss in Seattle. He owns the whole set-up – and a lot more besides. He owns firms in Alaska and California, as well as Washington.[26]

'The whole set-up – and a lot more besides' captures the logic of possession nicely: the romantic hero owns everthing and more. His possessions are the visible signs of a wealth without limit, just as his physical strength is the visible sign of immeasurable power. His authority pervades the world:

> ... Jarret Earle had the air of a man who knew what he wanted and had no intention of being intimidated by anyone in the process. Airport formalities held neither mystery nor hold-ups for him, and in a crowd his was the eye of authority that always commanded – and got – attention ...[27]

Capital is an aspect of the romantic hero's power, and the romantic hero's power is an aspect of capital. He restores its mystique. One of the rewards of the heroine's trial is to enter into an alliance with this wealth-machine. Here, we can see, in more detail, how the heroine's function is to join Foucault's two deployments of alliance and sexuality. The romantic hero is a fantastical personification of the deployment of sexuality, 'proliferating, innovating, annexing, creating, and penetrating bodies in increasingly detailed ways'. The heroine's task is to harness this energy to the deployment of alliance, which has an inbuilt tendency to fixation, mere repetition.[28] She does this where others have tried and failed: a typical story is one where the hero's dark secret is a failed marriage, and the marriage has failed because the woman did not honour the obligations of the deployment of alliance. Very often she has abused the power of the hero's name by committing adultery. The heroine learns about the secret – it is one moment when she sees through the hero after all his seeing through her – and offers him the reassurance of her absolute dependence, the dependence which romantic fiction labels love. If her desire needs dependence as its condition, so does his love. He needs to learn that she really is that dependent, that she won't pursue a career or another man, so that he can love her on the model of a father's love for a daughter. The chamber of horrors is transformed into a garden of earthly delights.

The fictional father is alive and well in modern

romance. He appears in the guise of the romantic hero. Because he is a fictional father and not a real one, he is not subject to the incest taboo. He can be desired and married. Popular romance bears an analogy to what Freud called the family romance, the tendency he discerned in children to at first enormously overvalue their parents, imagining them as king and queen, and then, as a more critical view develops out of rivalry and disappointment, to undervalue them.[29] Mills and Boon stories reverse this process from the daughter's perspective. Starting from a point of relative disenchantment, the romantic hero recreates the terms of the daughter's first enchanted view of the father. The heroine is relieved from the anxiety of growing up. She can stay a daughter in an infantile story for grown-ups. Freud's name for the process typified by this kind of story was regression, a means of coping with anxiety by returning to an earlier stage of development.

Regression usually carries a critical edge to it, implying that someone has failed to be what she should. Romantic fiction can be, and has been, judged to be regressive from other perspectives than those of psycho-analysis. Enter the furrowed brow of the critical intellectual: 'romantic fiction reproduces patriarchal and capitalist ideologies'. But it's not simply a question of reproducing these ideologies; romantic fiction revels in them: male sexuality may threaten violence but that is the necessary prelude to bliss. Forget the degradations of capitalism and enjoy all the wealth it produces. Romantic fiction thus appears to subvert the critical intellectual's best hopes of a just future. This becomes the starting point for another intellectual stance, an alternative to the first. Detecting the authoritarianism implicit in the first view, a more generous view invites us to celebrate the products of popular culture, to cherish popular pleasures and learn from them. There is nothing new in this division of attitudes.

In writing about romantic fiction, or any other popular form, it is difficult not to fall into one of these two positions, or to unknowingly shuttle between them. In place of a resolution of this dilemma, I offer a hypothesis and a wish.

The hypothesis is that modern romantic fiction can be seen as a product of that sector of the culture industry whose concern is the manufacture of glamour. A minimum specification of glamour would include the following: that the glamorous world is a dream, but one which might turn out to be true or imitable; that glamour makes abstract properties – power, purity, corruption and so on – into visible character or scene; that identity is based upon a mirror (you are as others see you); and that glamour is nostalgic, attracted to forms of power which are in decline or have become marginal. Glamour is an effect which can be found in soap operas like *Dallas* and *Dynasty* – paternal narratives both – and in romantic fiction. It is the lurid glow given off by a rotting object.[30] In a period when actual paternal power has retreated into the family – often with disastrous results, as the father compensates for his weakness in the outside world by victimising the family he regards as his own – *Dallas, Dynasty* and romantic fiction project the father as a power in the great world, a visible sovereign to be challenged and adored. In Foucault's terms, these forms recreate the sovereign figure of ancient power amidst the trappings of modern power. They are fuelled by a nostalgia to make power visible.

My wish is to have done with fictional fathers, with that whole tradition of figuring the father as a monster or god. It is a pious wish, of course, a vestige of humanism. Kafka, who knew more about fathers than most, tried to come to terms with his, to talk to him as one human being to another. But, of course, he could not *talk* to him. That would have led to a row. So he wrote him a letter instead. It soon grew monstrous, more than forty pages long.[31] The letter suggests that Kafka wanted to be reasonable. He wants to find his independence, but not through a rebellion which will sever all contact with his father. But something else happens, the old murderous logic which eludes rational, justice-seeking intentionality, and, in writing his letter, Kafka starts to reproduce his father's power, not to address him as an equal. Is that Kafka's way of gaining power over his father, by reinventing him? Or does it show his father's power over him, that he cannot invent anything else? An unanswerable question. The letter was never sent.

Notes

[1] S Freud, *Totem and Taboo*, in *The Standard Edition of the Complete Psychological Works of Sigmund Freud* (hereafter referred to as Standard Edition), Vol 13, edited and translated by J Strachey, Hogarth Press, 1955, pp.144-45.

[2] S Freud, *Moses and Monotheism*, Standard Edition, Vol 23 (1964), pp.87-88.

[3] For an accessible reproduction of *Saturn Eating his Children* see K Clark, *The Romantic Rebellion*, John Murray/Sotheby, Parke, Bernet, London 1973, p.93.

[4] For reproductions of the pictures referred to here see R Klibansky, E Panofsky, F Saxl, *Saturn and Melancholy*, Nelson, London 1964, plates 46, 47, 48, 49, 52.

[5] S Freud, *Totem and Taboo*, p.156.

[6] *Ibid*, p.50.

[7] For an example see the treatment of Casaubon and his death in George Eliot's *Middlemarch*.

[8] S Freud, *Totem and Taboo*, pp.149-50.

[9] A Wilden, *System and Structure*, Tavistock Publications, London 1972, Chapter 5; for an influential predecessor to Wilden in thinking about the double-bind see G Bateson, 'Towards a Theory of Schizophrenia' (first published in 1956), in *Steps Towards an Ecology of Mind*, Intertext Books, 1972, pp.201-228.

[10] G W F Hegel, *The Phenomenology of Mind*, Harper Colophon Books, New York 1967, p 226.

[11] J Hyppolite, *Studies on Marx and Hegel*, Harper Torchbooks, New York 1969, p.162.

[12] For a fuller analysis of the master/slave dialectic see Charles Taylor, *Hegel*, Cambridge University Press 1975, pp.153-7.

[13] For a reproduction of *The Third of May 1808*, see K Clark, *op cit*, p.86.

[14] J Lacan, *Ecrits*, Le Seuil, Paris 1966, p.556, cited in A Wilden, *op cit*, p.281.

[15] M Foucault, *The History of Sexuality*, Pelican 1981, part 5: Right of Death and Power Over Life.

[16] *Ibid*, p.106.

[17] *Ibid*, p.106.

[18] *Ibid*, p.113.

[19] N West, *Devil's Gold*, Mills and Boon 1982, p.5. I have found some of the work in the following books valuable for thinking about popular romantic fiction: T Modleski, *Loving with a Vengeance*, Methuen 1985, and J Radford (ed), *The Progress of Romance*, Routledge and Kegan Paul, 1986.

[20] M Hilton, *Snow Bride* Mills and Boon 1979, p.12.

[21] *Ibid*, p.189.

[22] *Ibid*, p.127.

[23] N West, *op cit*, p.95.

[24] M Hilton, *op cit*, p.80.

[25] M Ker, *Ice Princess*, Mills and Boon 1985, p.97.

[26] N West, *op cit*, p.51.

[27] M Hilton, *op cit*, p.30.

[28] For a parallel discussion of *Dombey and Son*, see, R Clark, 'Riddling the Family Firm: The Sexual Economy of Dombey and Son'. In *ELH*, Vol 51, 1984, pp.69-84.

[29] For Freud's account of the family romance, see Standard Edition, Volume 9, (1959), pp.235-241.

[30] My brief discussion of the meanings of glamour can be set alongside the comments by John Berger in *Ways of Seeing*: 'The happiness of being envied is glamour ... The power of the glamorous resides in their supposed happiness ... It is this which explains the absent, unfocussed look of so many glamour images. They look out over the looks of envy which sustain them.' J Berger, *Ways of Seeing*, BBC/Penguin 1972, pp.132-133.

[31] For the text of Kafka's letter in translation, see F Kafka, *Dearest Father*, Schocken Books, New York, 1954, pp.138-198.

On Becoming a Lesbian Reader

ALISON HENNEGAN

Sometime in 1960 my mother and I had a brief and civilised altercation in a newsagent's near the junction of the Strand and Northumberland Avenue. I stood beside a revolving bookstand and said, defiant but confused, 'I want *this* one'. I went on saying it for several minutes as she, gently, reasonably, worriedly and, in the end, successfully, explained to me that I didn't, not *really*, not if I thought about it properly. It cost half-a-crown and I only had five shillings to spend. We'd only just got off the train and had a whole day ahead of us: who knew what other books I'd see later and would want even more? ('But', I muttered, 'I want *this* one.') And anyway, she continued, it didn't really look a very *nice* book, did it? The two women on the front looked … well … they didn't look … well … the whole *thing* looked rather … well … *sordid*, didn't I think?

She was quite right: it did. With shaky draughtsmanship and lurid colours some harassed hack had dashed off a wildly inaccurate 'impression' of an 1890s Paris bar. Unnaturally blonde, alarmingly dentifriced, two women sprawled across a table and each other, hair, eyes and teeth all straight off a 1950s pin-up calendar. Pretty nasty. ('But I want *this* one …')

I didn't buy it and remember nothing of the rest of the day. Looking back I've become confused about whether the book, hideously bedizened, poor thing, was Daudet's *Sapho* or Zola's *Nana*. But, either way, distinctly classy reading really, and just the thing, if a little precocious, for a twelve-year-old upwardly mobile grammar school girl with (at that time) Oxford ambitions. Had its cover been more restrained – a tasteful green and white like the Penguin French Classics of the day, perhaps – I might have bought it with pleasure, profit and approval.

I find the incident illuminating. I remember it, for a start, more than a quarter of a century later. And, looking back, it seems to me to combine so many elements which marked my uncertain progress as a youthful lesbian reader. It evoked so many powerful but mixed emotions. Panic, at the prospect of the book slipping through my hands. An angry sense of shame, unbidden, resented and uncomprehended. Bewilderment at the intensity of my conviction that *this* was the book I wanted, even though author and title signified nothing to me then. Fear, lest by forcing the issue I should anger and distance my mother. Distress that my somehow necessary, albeit eventually defeated, intransigence should distress her. All in all it was an eventful five minutes.

Over the years all those responses would become familiar, recognised more quickly, understood more clearly. Some (shame, fear) would vanish altogether. Another – that curious, instant certainty of knowledge that a particular book, poem, author was one of 'mine' – would grow, throwing up its own endlessly fascinating questions about how it is and what it is that we 'read'.

Like many young lesbians and gay men I became adept at finding 'my' books, often in unlikely places (in a London newsagent's at the junction of the Strand and Northumberland Avenue, for example). I became aware of and learned to rely on a phenomenon which I can only call a pricking of my thumbs, a capacity which led me, unfailingly and time and time again, to the 'right' book for me, however unlikely its disguise.

Friends and enemies who prize rationality above all else hate it when I talk about my thumbs: they believe it brings criticism into disrepute. But I continue unrepentantly. The phrase is shorthand for that mysterious process whereby the searching eye rapidly and unerringly isolates those elements – identified in a particular publisher's colophon, in chapter headings, in an author's photograph or coded biographical note, in the identity of a series editor, in the cumulative effect of a writer's previous publications listed in the front – which suggest that *this* book might repay examination. The pricking of my thumbs is akin to 'woman's instinct': no genetically determined, paranormal power but a complex and subtle system of noticing and connecting a myriad of facts usually deemed irrelevant or insignificant.

If my language suggests a mixture of the hunting field and the mystery novel, with me doubling as whipper-in and Hawkshaw the Detective and the books cast as my elusive quarry, that's probably just how it should be. Any teenager in search of lesbian popular fiction in 1960 was in trouble. There wasn't any – or not, at least, in any sense we'd recognise today. The teenage 'problem' novel, which now feels able to deal with broken marriages, divorce, wife-battering, incest, rape, schoolgirl pregnancy, abortion, drug abuse and madness, scarcely existed. A decorous silence was maintained on the subject of adolescent sexuality, let alone homosexuality. Had I been a little older, a little more sophisticated, a little closer to London, I might have tracked down the odd paperback novel by Ann Bannon, *Women of the Shadows* or *Odd Girl Out*, perhaps. But Bannon didn't make it to the bookshops of Epsom and Leatherhead and, anyway, financial constraints and personal inclination tended to limit me to the second-hand and to the cheaper end of the antiquarian market. Bannon would come later. 'Gay' wasn't there as a term, yet, and for many lesbians 'lesbian' was a word arousing terror, self-hatred and contempt.

I didn't know that. At twelve I didn't even know the word. I wasn't clear who I was yet, but I had inklings. I knew that the figure of Nancy Spain, with her uncoiffeured hair, well cut hacking jacket, open-necked shirt and rakish cravat, gave me a warm glow as I watched her on *Juke Box Jury* but I didn't know why. And I knew that her weekly cross-talk act with Gilbert Harding, who always sat next to her on *What's My Line?*, gave me the same comforted pleasure, but I couldn't explain it. Now, of course, I know that they were having a whale of a time playing at being a flirtatious heterosexual couple, enacting an outrageously camp open secret. It was fun, it was flagrant, and utterly unperceived by the bulk of their audience. Very Firbank, I would realise later.

Sometimes, I knew, books gave me something of that same ill defined warmth and pleasure. And, I began to realise, it was a pleasure which I increasingly needed and sought. It wasn't easy to define at first, which made it difficult to seek it out, and made even stranger that sudden flash of recognition sparked by a particular book.

Sometimes the elusive and desired quality seemed easier to define negatively. There were various things it was not, various states in which it could not exist. It was not to be found where women characters were happily dependent on men or where a man or marriage and children were offered as women's rightful destiny. It fled whenever the central female character with whom the author demanded I identify was desirable, beautiful or thin. Women's erotic power for me, I gradually and painfully recognised, was at that time rooted in my own sense of (inferior) difference from them. I could and did desire them but could not, like them, be desired. If, however, the author permitted me, or, indeed, instructed me as reader to desire a female character, I still had problems. In the popular fiction of my childhood, those who desired women were men. Working out that it wasn't necessarily so occupied most of my adolescence. Trying to decide what to do with that knowledge took most of my early womanhood.

One of the reasons why it took so long was that my usual allies let me down. Like many children born to elderly parents, books were my chief companions, my most important source of knowledge. Yet in them I could find no explanation of the thing I sought, even if I sometimes found the thing itself. Today, aided by an extensive body of gay and feminist criticism, I can say, if I choose to, that my needs and demands as an adolescent reader demonstrated an obvious anxiety and ambivalence about my traditionally narrowly defined gender role, allied to uncertainty about my developing and clearly lesbian sexual identity. Basically, although I didn't realize it, I was looking for books which would help me recognise, respect and enact my sexuality. Those critics say it nicely, in a friendly fashion, but no one was saying it then. Psychiatrists *were* saying something similar in a distinctly unfriendly and disapproving fashion but, mercifully, I knew nothing of it.

Somehow I had to find my own solution. That books should be unable, or, even worse, unwilling to help me was unthinkable. Somehow I had to find a way of reading *round* those elements I rejected whilst discovering a means of reading my way *to* the ones I needed and increasingly suspected must be there in *some* books, *some*where. If they were there, I must find them. And if they weren't? Then I must make them, not by writing my own books but by reading in a way which forced character, theme and plot to yield every last scrap of knowledge and perception which they might offer for the solution of this central but nebulous mystery.

In other words, I did as most young gay and lesbian readers of the time – older ones, too, for that matter – had to do. I created my own 'popular fiction', developed my own much cherished canon. (Many years later I discovered that Edward Carpenter, impelled by just such a need and writing for others who felt it too, had compiled his own collection of valued extracts, drawing upon the literature of the ancient world, mediaeval and Renaissance Europe and his own day. He published it in 1902 as *Ioläus: An Anthology of Friendship*.)

The relations of my personal literary canon to other, more orthodox ones were quixotic. Sometimes it overlapped with them (Homer and Austen), sometimes diverged (Blyton and Brazil) or ran underground, out of sight (Walford and Warboise. *Who?* WARBOISE, Jane, Mrs). And sometimes it marched side by side, parallel but mocking (as in 'You read *your* Dickens and I'll read *mine!*'). The quest (and that word, so evocative of perils and prizes, dangers and delights, is apt) for books which would provide that sense of warmth, comfort, recognition and inclusion, took me into many areas not usually deemed 'popular'. I might never have found them had the day's popular fiction not let me down so badly. Ironically, therefore, I must presumably rejoice that it did.

That I turned early to ancient Greece need come as no surprise. If there's one thing everyone knows about the Greeks it's that they were all That Way. Even *I* knew that much. Yet because they were so thoroughly dead, so safely Then rather than dangerously Now, even quite strict grown-ups seemed to regard the Greeks with relieved approval. These days I'm told it's 'elitist' to know classical Greek. If that means that the ever rarer ability to read it opens up a magnificently rich and vibrant world, a deeply desirable source of pleasure and delight, I'd agree, although it's always seemed to me a reason for keeping it on the curriculum rather than hissing it off. But in my early teens 'elitism' did not yet exist: unguilty, I headed hastily for a literature and a world which I confidently expected to find emotionally more congenial, more recognisable, more illuminating than my teenage present.

And so I did. That women's own voices were virtually silent, bar a few precious scraps of lyric poetry and the occasional verbatim transcript from a court hearing, did not then worry me. What I was looking for were strong and passionate emotions which bound human beings to members of their own sex rather than to the other. That the bonds depicted existed primarily between men didn't matter. In part this was because I spent at least half my adolescence 'being male' inside my own head: 'gender identity confusion' in today's terminology, or 'male identified', but neither phrase is right or adequate. I never for one moment thought I was a man nor wished to be. But somehow I had to find a way of thinking of myself which included the possibility of desiring women. And those who desire women are men. (See above.)

And just exactly how, you might well ask, did a passionate identification with an Achilles distraught with grief at the death of his beloved Patroclus help me towards a recognition that women, too, may desire women?

It did it by offering me a world free from the assumption that human completeness exists solely in the fusion of male and female. Implicitly, the *Iliad* – and Plato's Socratic dialogues, and the *Antigone*, and the Greek Anthology's paederastic love poems, and Theocritos's *Idylls*, and ... and ... and ... – refused to be bound by the belief that true psychological maturity, personal fulfil-ment and social worth existed only in heterosexuality, marriage and parenthood. Not that they despised those things, either: they simply declined to elevate them at the cost of all else. And that, for me, was freedom indeed.

I came to believe, and to a large extent still do, that hostility to homosexuality stems mainly from a widespread and deeply rooted desire for polarity. It's no accident that 'Opposites attract' is used neutrally or approvingly whereas 'Birds of a feather ...', which asserts the attraction of like to like, is invariably used pejoratively. A dualistic belief in the Male and Female Principles underpins so much of our thinking, whether we're dealing with mediaeval cosmogonies or behavioural psychology, Renaissance theories of grammar or modern genetics. In sexual terms, it is most frequently translated into an implicit demand that we should desire and value Otherness, reject and despise Sameness or Self. Remem-ber how long and how happily mainstream psychiatry condemned all homosexuality as basically 'narcissistic'. Remember too, with gratitude, how clearly the early gay liberationists recognised that a theory which damns as 'immature' the capacity to love a body formed in one's own image is a theory rooted in self-hatred.

I know that in many ways my Greeks were an undesirable lot. I know that slavery supported their Glory and that the male bonding I celebrate was often accompanied by a corresponding belittling of women. I know. Nevertheless, at a time when I desperately needed it, they were the only ones to offer me the vision of a world which acknowledged – rejoiced, even – that the ties uniting people of the same sex are frequently, in part, erotic.

'*My* Greeks', I say, affectionately proprietorial, but perfectly aware that my possessiveness betrays me. They are – these happily homosexual heroes, philosophers and poets – my own creation, moulded lovingly to my own needs. They are a fiction whom I 'write' for myself. In just the same way, I later learned, generations of 19th century scholars, divines, teachers and authors wrote their own versions of ancient Greece. Many of them were homosexual too, drawn as I had been by a world which seemed to offer space for otherwise unhouseable emotions. Their sermons, poems, essays and historical novels, celebrating an 'earlier' world which they were themselves in the act of creating, taught me something of the present's power to change the past, taught me a little of the nature of 'History', 'Truth' and fiction.

Even more important, perhaps, I recognised the urgency and passion which informed their recreation of the ancient world. These men, like me, were asking to be included in literature, demanding that there at least they should be able to find and respect their own needs, emotions and experience. They and I, however unlikely it might seem, formed part of a common readership who, united by one overriding need, could to a remarkable extent transcend our differences of gender, class and time. With and through those beleaguered Victorians I learned yet another lesson about the unexpected nature of loyalty and allegiance. Many things about those men I might dislike, even loathe. But I could never overlook that basic affinity rooted in our shared and stigmatised love for members of our own sex. I recognised them as members of 'my people'. It was my own crude and early version of 'a gay identity' before any of us knew the thing existed. A decade later, in a much more sophisticated form shared with thousands of others, it would help to create a movement, a press, a theory of sexual politics and a thriving community of openly gay authors writing for openly gay readers.

But at that earlier stage I was content to follow the tracks left by my Victorian proto-gay predecessors. And they too, I discovered, had had their own spiritual ancestors. Georgians, Jacobeans, Elizabethans, twelfth-century monks and the occasional nun, had all been there before us, avidly scrutinising Greece and Rome for any vestige of recognisable emotions. The references weren't always flattering. Catullus and Martial were often spiteful, Juvenal was uniformly vile. But Petronius's light hearted paederasty, Horace's urbane bisexuality, Virgil's occasional elegaic homo-eroticism and Lucian's elegant lesbians all helped. My Latin and Greek improved, too. Even when I was cheating with reprints of some of the truly magnificent 16th and 17th century translations, a modern editor had invariably decided that *some* passages really *must* remain in the decent obscurity of a learned language. Somehow the bits *I* needed never quite made it into English. Nothing for it but to grapple with the original. Almost incidentally I ended up with quite a respectable working knowledge of The Development of the Ancient Novel.

Even if they let me down at crucial moments, the translations taught me a great deal. They showed me, at first hand, how each age and generation sets its own revealing and distorting imprint on the works it forces into versions acceptable to itself. It was alarming but enlightening to watch a succession of late 19th and early 20th century men first translate Sappho's poems then tie themselves in knots as they attempted to explain away what they had just translated. It was sad but instructive to discover that some editor-translators weren't above changing the gender of a pronoun if the new reading suited contemporary morality better. It was an early and quickly grasped object lesson in the power wielded by those who establish and transmit texts. To watch what happened to Homeric warriors at the hands of Chapman, Pope, Arnold, Samuel Butler and T E Lawrence was its own fascinating lesson in the near impossibility of 'translating' anything truthfully from the past to the present.

Ripples from that lesson would go on spreading outwards. Later, as I wrestled with the shifts which had occurred over the centuries in the language used to describe love between women, I recognised the same problem. What did it *mean* when two 19th century women expressed their feelings for each other in the words of the marriage ceremony? What did it *mean* when one Bluestocking wrote to another that two mutual women friends had lost their hearts to each other and needed nothing more? What did it *mean* when one prim early Victorian spinster said to another that she could never be happy again until that moment when she felt once more her friend's lips upon her breast?

The vast mass of once popular, now neglected novels written by women during the 18th and 19th centuries offered occasional glimmerings. It wasn't the Greats – the Austens, Brontës, Gaskells and Eliots – I turned to here but the 'second rank': the Mrs Henry Woods, Charlotte M Yonges, Rosa Nouchette Careys, and a whole host of lesser sisters, the ones often dismissed as 'lady novelists' and writing primarily for women and teenage girls. (Not that you can ever trust those sniffy judgements. Whole regiments wept, we're told, when C M Yonge's heir of Redclyffe died.)

In these 'women's books', with their meticulously detailed accounts of a women's world, curious and suggestive tensions emerged. Theoretically, marriage and motherhood were presented as a woman's true destiny, the only true success. Yet the more 'womanly' the book, the less visible were male characters. The novels' real content lay in the women's interactions with each other: in the advice they gave, care they took, support they offered, sacrifices they made. Whatever the ideology lurking outside the sitting-room, on *this* side of the door things were far less clear. In novel after novel happy marriages would be brutally dissolved by sudden death, wretched ones dragged on interminably, dissolvable only by a death which never seemed to come. And many of the women never married anyway, whether for lack of opportunity or inclination. Before one's eyes, the norm – Happy Wife, Happy Mother – melted away. Was this Realism or Revolt, I wondered as I read.

Wherever I scented mutinous tendencies in an author, I helped them along a little by the creation of my own parallel text. And this was a liberty I felt as free to take with the Greats as with the Also-rans. Fanny Price was obviously never going to come to any good with Edmund

so I gave her to Mary Crawford instead and ended
Mansfield Park properly. Charlotte Lucas had to be saved
from Mr Collins somehow and Elizabeth Bennett seemed
to me to be the woman to do it. (Sometimes I let Darcy
have Bingley instead. If I was feeling really kind I
invented an entirely new character for him, someone with
Bingley's integrity and Wickham's profile.)

If a male novelist seemed to be teetering on the brink of
promising intimations I'd give him a helpful shove. *Our
Mutual Friend* was so clearly improved and rang truer, if
Eugene ended up with Mortimer, Lizzie with Bella. Miss
Abbey, redoubtable publican of the Thamesside Six Jolly
Fellowship-Porters, is obviously a dyke and deserves a
worthy lover. I gave her one. Clearly Steerforth should
live *and* have David Copperfield who's anyway been madly
in love with him from that first moment in the
playground. Thus should the world be ordered and thus I
ordered it. (By the time I came across Ronald Firbank I
saw at once that he had made an art form out of doing
pretty much the same thing: defiantly creating a world in
which characters got the partners *he* wanted them to have,
and stuff the rest of you.)

John Osborne, in a fit of pique, once said that reading
Gay News made him feel as though he were looking at the
world through the wrong end of a telescope. I knew
exactly what he meant because that was my experience too
as I read my way through endless heterosexual novels
which never seemed to acknowledge *my* perspective on the
world. Rewriting selected bits of Great Literature was my
way of adjusting the picture.

I didn't always have to change the picture. Sometimes all
I had to do was fill it in a little. As with school stories, for
example. Like the good parent she was and is, my mother
was worried to find the sixteen-year-old me still reading
Enid Blyton's Malory Towers books. (I was also reading
Dostoevsky, Stendhal and Flaubert, but still ...) Recently
browsing once more through Sheila Ray's *The Blyton
Phenomenon* I noted that reading surveys carried out
amongst schoolchildren reveal that it is those girls who are
academic high flyers who go on reading Enid Blyton's

school stories longest. The surveyors were surprised. I'm
not. Schoolgirls who spend long hours in their bedrooms
reading books are often schoolgirls who are desperately
trying to escape from schoolboys and there's many a baby
dyke amongst them. The much despised girls' school story
invariably offered an enclosed community entirely
governed and administered by women: none of this
rubbish about healthy co-educational establishments in
which – surprise, surprise – the Head Teacher just *happens*
to be male. In these stories casual communication with the
outside world is discouraged and made difficult. Flutters
of excitement over inaccessible boys are briskly dismissed
as 'silliness'. The teachers are qualified, proudly conscious
of professional status and invariably dedicated to a career
which they have chosen. Their single state is more a cause
for satisfaction than regret. The books might seem
repressive of female sexuality from a heterosexual
viewpoint. From my lesbian one they were perfection.
There was nothing I needed to filter out, nothing I had to
work hard to ignore. All I had to do was add, provide, as it
were, a subtext. So I did.

And, if truth be told, still do. Darrell Rivers defied all
my efforts. There is something quintessentially and
dispiritingly sexless about her. Sally, her best friend, on
the other hand... Horse-mad Bill (short for Wilhelmina)
and equally horse-mad (but also bewitchingly auburn
haired and green eyed) Clarissa obviously belonged
together which is where I put them. And, for the rest, the
six volumes (from trembling first former to lordly Head of
School) provided, provide, an endless supply of erotic
variables. I still collect older school stories, still keep an eye
on newer ones. I value particularly those whose authors
show an intelligent and subtle appreciation of their
characters' constantly developing sexual complexity.
Antonia Forest's Kingscote sequence seems to me
exemplary. Anne Digby's extremely popular, knowingly
sexy, boy-mad Trebizonians leave me cold.

The Blytons and Brazils were written for child readers.
There is, however, a whole vast subgenre of school stories
– boys' public school novels – written primarily for adults.

Arising sometime in the 1850s and beginning to gather momentum in the 70s and 80s, they flower magnificently from the turn of the century through to the mid-1930s. I discovered them early and they compel me still. They share features with the later, lesser girls' stories: most obviously in their single-sex enclosed communities with their strictly hierarchical structures. But these novels pose larger and more disquieting questions: however enclosed in time and space the communities which they depict may seem to be, events develop against a constant, foreshadowing awareness of the larger world which waits outside. The apparently self-referring, self-sufficient system of schoolboy morality and boy government is both a preparation for and a rejection of what lies ahead. The schoolboy code seems simple, expressing itself in a language richly compounded of the Three Fields – hunting, games and battle: never shirk your fences; keep a straight bat; fight to the last ditch. But the best of the novels acknowledge a tension between the simplicities of childhood's code and the coming complexity of adulthood. Will those simple rules see a man through life, and should they? Doubt is admitted into the schoolboy Eden.

Predictably, within this all-male world of boys taught by men, few topics generated more tension – in 19th century fact as well as fiction – than male love. The word 'homosexuality' was invented by a Swiss psychologist in 1869. It was a coinage reflecting and engendered by the period's increasing medical and philosophical anxiety about the nature and object of sexual desire. Over the next 60 years human sexuality would be fragmented in an endless proliferation of -isms, -philias, -ities and -sions. It was a period in which the rules and boundaries were changing constantly. A word, touch or gesture which in an earlier period expressed an uncomplicated and confident exchange of loving affection between men had become suspect and taboo a few decades later. Love between men – whether sexual or not – was becoming a Problem. And in institutions where several hundred adolescent boys were herded together, often for unbroken stretches of five or six months at a time ...? In life and novels Headmasters, teachers, parents and pupils wrestled with some of the ethical dilemmas produced by a system which sometimes seemed designed to teach the very 'vice' it feared.

What, I wanted to know, was life like for my Victorians caught in the crossfire of rapid cultural change? Who were the boys these men had been? How had they formed their sense of self? Which elements in the attitudes and arguments surrounding their adolescence had made it easier or harder to reach some degree of understanding and acceptance of their own sexual natures? (And, always, nagging away in the background, what might they have to teach me?)

Factual evidence is scanty. Few surviving diaries offer us the devastating frankness and brutal self-revelation of the adolescent Harrovian, John Addington Symonds. All his hopeless confusion, guilt and self-hatred was projected, with disastrous results, upon the Headmaster whom he loathed himself for loving. Such first-hand accounts are rare indeed. But in the novels, many of them written by men who had good cause to know that not all 'phases' are merely 'passing', I could feel something of the psychological stress and turmoil of those endless emotional and sexual double-binds imposed upon the children of the junior forms, the adolescents of the Remove and the young men of the Sixth.

Imposed, too, upon many of their adult teachers. Novels and light verse of the period are full of the yearning but rigorously controlled love of older men for their youthful and swiftly passing charges. The situation is itself at best a cliché, at worst a dirty joke. I found it neither. As I read the autobiographies and memoirs which complemented the poetry and fiction, I gradually pieced together a significant portion of the emotional map of 19th century English schooling. Here indeed was a Sentimental Education and one in which much of the finest and most valued teaching proved to be the expression of some of the most despised emotions. Long before I knew the words 'repression', 'sublimation', and 'transference', the experiences of these men (women, too, I later discovered as I learned more about the development of girls' education) forced me to think about human arithmetic. What is lost when sexuality is denied its most obvious expression? What may be gained when it's compelled to express itself more obliquely? And how do you do that sum, how make yourself the actuary of your own emotions?

Sometimes the sum seemed savagely easy. In rage and fury I rewrote novels – and real lives – in a frenzy of prodigal giving. For every loving Housemaster there was a Golden Boy, for each fine teacher sacked ('… regretfully I have decided to accept his resignation …') there was grovelling apology, reinstatement and professional honour.

But sometimes I couldn't do the sum at all, couldn't even identify and separate the units I was supposed to be adding or subtracting, multiplying or dividing. Has the sex 'gone' simply because you refuse to touch the beloved you teach? Have you purged or purified your Impurity, reformed or transformed it, destroyed or recreated it? I was as confused as the period itself. And small wonder, given the question which both it and I were really asking. What actually, we wanted to know, *is* sex? I found no answer then, have found no fully satisfactory one since. But gradually I realised that being able to ask the question must mean that there was and is no single, self-evident solution. That, in itself, was an advance. And one which helped me to begin to make sense of Siegfried Sassoon and Wilfred Owen.

In the War of 1914-18, the Great War, I was to discover, for the last time, yet another of those vast male worlds whose literature drew me, and drew from me a passionate response grounded in that elusive but powerful sense of recognition and emotional affinity. When I was fourteen, knowing virtually nothing of the First World War other than that it had happened and life had never been the same again, I came across Sassoon's poem, 'The Dug Out', and, by the pricking of my thumbs recognised it and him as 'mine': –

Why do you lie with your legs ungainly huddled,
And one arm bent across your sullen, cold,
Exhausted face? It hurts my heart to watch you,
Deep-shadow'd from the candle's guttering gold;
And you wonder why I shake you by the shoulder;

Drowsy, you mumble and sigh and turn your head …
You are too young to fall asleep for ever;
And when you sleep you remind me of the dead.

Shortly afterwards Owen brought me that same thrill of certainty. Fifteen years later I watched, amused but incredulous, as certain sections of the critical establishment recoiled in horrified disbelief that anyone should profane Owen's name by pointing to the homo-eroticism which suffuses his poetry and shaped his life.

That war, as I experienced it through the words of the men who fought it, forced upon me some of the most difficult and disturbing lessons. Owen's ceaseless and anguished battle to reconcile the joint impulses to love and kill men exemplified the cruel contradictions at the heart of the warrior caste. (Echoes, once more, of the *Iliad*....) Daily, men endured appalling conditions with astonishing stoicism, dealt compassionately with weaker comrades, ran most terrible risks to retrieve the wounded, showed a loving, tender patience to the dying. Men trapped by inhuman circumstances frequently achieved superhuman feats of generosity and endurance. From all that was vile came much that was magnificent. Yet the love which found such unexpected expression was called into being by a convulsive collision of nation states hell-bent on each other's destruction. When men love their comrades most, they hate the enemy best. Love and hate become hopelessly entangled, mutually dependent: each becomes the expression of the other. In Owen's work that intolerable tension produces magnificent poetry. The man who was a savagely courageous fighter did not deceive himself about the links between lust and blood-lust ('… for each man kills the thing he loves …', as an earlier, less bellicose gay poet had observed). Owen recognised that, sometimes, killing men can seem to be the only way to kill the desire you feel for them and are afraid to feel.

He recognised other things, too. Such a shameful waste of loving was rooted in spurious concepts of Manhood, seductively clothed in the devastatingly glamorous accoutrements of Honour and Chivalry. Truly fine things

– courage, gallantry, stamina – were dangerously confused with baser ones. It's one thing to endure pain and suffering for a worthy end. To 'pass the pain barrier' simply to win a race is quite another. The cult of male athleticism which began to spread so fast during the late 19th century and which ended by making the whole world into one vast sportsground on which to play 'The Great Game of Life', was a cult strongly tinged with unacknowledged masochism and desire. It offered men the only acceptable way of recognising and pursuing male physical beauty – their own and other men's. But the body was both revered and punished, *must* indeed be punished – with rigorous diet, exercise and denial – to make it worthy of reverence – hard, fit, victorious. The body was as much enemy as ally. It must be controlled and, ultimately, conquered. It was and was not oneself. In a period which had outlawed sexual love between men, it was inevitable that men's relations with their own bodies would become tormentingly difficult, an impossible fusion of love and loathing, fear and pride. And if you may not love your own male body uncomplicatedly, what hope is there of finding a way to acknowledge and express your love and desire for those whose bodies are the same as yours? War, Owen suggested, is what happens when men are too frightened to face the love they feel for each other. The Great War was, in part, the inevitable outcome of the perplexities and confusions which had so exercised my Victorian schoolboys, but this time it was confusion on a spectacular scale of horror. Many of those same schoolboys perished in it.

Owen made the connections in a body of work that ranks amongst the finest thrown up by that or any other war. But there were others making them, too, not least amongst the many homosexual men and women who set their face against the bloodshed and formed or joined groups lobbying for a negotiated peace.

For some five years I collected avidly every book I could find about the Great War, concentrating always on those written during the war itself or in the immediate aftermath. I amassed volumes of autobiography, memoir, polemic, propaganda, poetry and fiction. Always, as I read, I found myself facing, and sometimes hating, my own conflicting responses. I *envied* – and was deeply ashamed of envying – the emotional closeness born of extremity which those men had known. I was appalled to realise that suffering on such a scale exerted an attraction for me which was quite certainly in part erotic. And I was infuriated at being forced to admit that for me, even for *me*, the panoply of war – the uniforms, bugles, banners, swords and horses, the whole arrogant display of chivalric machismo – was deeply exciting in a way which was undeniably sexual. I didn't like discovering any of that. But better to know it than not, and better to confess to it at once so that I could try to understand and deal with it.

The writings of the Great War represented, as I have said, the last literary male world in which I would immerse myself. I was learning of others all the time and explored them as thoroughly as I could, but none of them held me as firmly as the War had done and continues to do. Nevertheless I was delighted to make my new discoveries, to extend my gay literary map, to forage through the nations and centuries discovering my forebears.

It was a curiously lurching progress, a serendipitous game of Hide and Seek where the only clues came from occasional hints dropped casually but discreetly by helpful teachers, from playground gossip, from the odd footnote in biographies, from the intricate system of coded cross reference and allusion embedded in the works of writers I had already recognised as 'mine' or sympathetic to me. Sometimes I expended enormous amounts of energy in 'discoveries' which should have been common knowledge. (I knew quite early on that Oscar Wilde had been imprisoned for *some*thing. It took a surprisingly long time before I could find anyone who'd tell me why. Apparently it was a matter of *such* common knowledge, it never needed to be said.)

By various hazardous routes I reached Marlowe, Bacon and Barnefield, Montaigne and Etienne de la Boétie, Rochester (and Savile?), Aphra Behn and her Clarinda. I found groups: Bluestockings in late 18th century England,

Hellenists in early 19th century Austria, assorted English exiles in mid-century Florence, *fin-de-siècle* poets in Paris. I encountered charismatic figures who attracted acolytes: Whitman in America, Wilde in London, Stefan George in Germany. I stumbled on loners out on a limb and tripped – didn't we all? – over Bloomsbury. There were the bad – Byron, Corvo, Rimbaud and Verlaine, half of Capri – and the sad – Charlotte Mew and Alfred Douglas – and the virtuous – Goldsworthy, Lowes, Dickinson, Edward Carpenter and Robert Ross.

There are two things you should notice about that list. Most of them are male and all of them are dead. In literature (as, at that time, in life) finding lesbians was hard. Finding live ones was very difficult. It's true that at that stage I was, curiously but commonly enough, almost happier with gay male protagonists. Paradoxically it was precisely because I so desperately wanted to find lesbians in literature that success could be frightening. I was placing such an impossible weight of expectation on those fictional characters, demanding that they reveal and represent so much. How could any one woman, real or imagined, provide everything that I was looking for? It was my own personal version of a problem which, in later years, a whole gay readership would present to its gay authors. Time and again gay novelists and dramatists whom I interviewed for the original *Gay News* would complain that gay readers and audiences seemed to expect that each gay character should be perfection, accused authors who depicted them as less than wholly admirable of 'self-oppression'. The demand was an index of our earlier deprivation: we asked so much of our precious fictional gay people because we had had so few of them. Even when I *had* braced myself to face another lesbian in fiction, to find her had always remained a challenge. (It took me, for instance, a long time to acknowledge that women had fought that Great War, too – as doctors, nurses, munitions workers, pacifists and even, in the case of the remarkable Flora Sandes, as a sergeant in the Serbian army. But it took me even longer to discover that many of them were lesbians. Fiction's most notorious lesbian, Stephen Gordon, hero/ine of Radclyffe Hall's 1928 *The Well of Loneliness*, had driven her ambulance through Flanders, but there were others lurking in less celebrated novels, such as Helen Smith's *Not So Quiet ... [on the Western Front]*.)

In many ways the problem of literature's Invisible Lesbians is simply the problem of women's writing writ large. I was searching before the most recent wave of feminism had produced its women's presses dedicated to reprinting and commissioning women's work. The bulk of women's lives go ignored, unknown, unrecorded. Women's lives are too 'trivial', 'boring', 'narrowly domestic' to matter and the novels which depict them are equally expendable. The fate of my 19th century lady novelists had taught me that. I found the worlds they created riveting, the morality they revealed fascinating, the dilemmas they described recognisable and moving. I also thought many of them extremely well written. But mainstream criticism ignores them, doesn't even seem to know that half of them exist. It was, I think, Mark Twain who came right out with it and said that he found Jane Austen's novels boring because there were no heroes, only heroines, and he just couldn't bear it. Over the years I've come to the conclusion that many critical works and theories which, by ignoring women's writing, implicitly assert the superiority of men's are using criteria no more sophisticated or laudable than Twain's: they just take more and longer words to say it.

By those standards lesbians are both more boring (no men) and more interesting (as in 'Hmmm, *INT*eresting!') than 'ordinary' (or 'real') women. Men's basic inability to believe in a form of sexuality which excludes them has always encouraged them to regard lesbianism as some elaborate cock-tease, a make-believe world of imaginary emotions and simulated sex. Confusingly, of course, men's basic ability to believe only too well and worriedly in a form of sexuality which excludes them has also encouraged them to regard lesbianism as necessary Extra Rations for the gender whose terrifying insatiability is well known. (The first literary lesbians I encountered, all male creations, were Juvenal's shrieking, sex-crazed harridans, Lucian's world-weary whores entertaining themselves between clients, and Brantôme's over-excited Ladies of the Court who'd just discovered something frightfully interesting about female weasels.)

All this tended to mean that the only lesbians who made it into fiction were either heavily disguised (and therefore virtually invisible) or alarmingly noticeable (and therefore rather frightening to a reader like myself seeking reassurance). The disguised ones led pale, chlorotic existences on the fringes of other people's lives. They were usually attached passionately but asexually and insecurely to larger, flamboyant and invariably heterosexual characters who took them for granted but never really noticed them. By the end of the book they were always demoralised, sometimes denounced and frequently discarded. Of course, when I say 'denounced' I refer to nothing so helpfully unambiguous as 'You're just a pathetic old dyke! Now get out!' I mean that various characters would go into a sibillant little huddle and mutter nastily about 'morbid sentimentality', 'unwise friendships' and the problems of 'superfluous women'. The noticeable ones got drunk a lot, beat up their girlfriends, either wore drag or were unbelievably elegant in *haute couture*, had breakdowns, broke furniture, played fast and loose, killed people sometimes, suffered a lot but never really even *began* to understand the meaning of the word 'love'.

Where, I wondered miserably, did the authors *find* these women? It was, of course, the key question. I was awfully slow to work it out (but then, there weren't too many people around to help at the time). Unbelievably naive though it must now sound, it really hadn't occurred to me that one of 'my' books might be written by the enemy. Gradually, punch drunk and reeling in a fictional world filled with 'lesbians' who were variously monstrous, freakish, ludicrous, contemptible, and just occasionally, utterly familiar and perfectly credible, I began to see daylight. 'Lesbians' could be created by:

(a)   a hostile but ignorant man (homo-, hetero- or bisexual)

(b)   a hostile but knowledgeable man (homo-, hetero- or
       bisexual)
(c)   a sympathetic but ill informed man (homo-, hetero- or
       bisexual)
(d)   a sympathetic and knowledgable man (homo-, hetero-
       or bisexual)
(e)   a hostile and ignorant heterosexual woman
(f)   a hostile and knowledgable heterosexual woman
(g)   a sympathetic but ill informed heterosexual woman
(h)   a sympathetic and well informed heterosexual woman
(i)   a hostile bisexual woman
(j)   a sympathetic bisexual woman
(k)   a screwed up lesbian
(l)   an OK lesbian

And, just in case things got too easy, some authors kept
switching categories. Baudelaire and Verlaine, for
instance, could be (b) *and* (d). Some began their careers as
(k) and ended them as (l). Some were (l) when they wrote
about gay men but become (k) when they wrote about
lesbians. And sometimes you suspected a writer was
pretending to be (f) or (h) when she was really (k). Molly
Keane was (e) in 1934 when she wrote *Devoted Ladies* but
grew up fast enough to have become (h) by 1937 when she
published *The Rising Tide*.

Once I'd worked all that out, lots of things became much
clearer quite quickly. And once I realised that the critics
who assessed 'my' books could also be classified in the same
way as their creators I began to understand how, for
example, one ludicrously insulting and laughably inade-
quate portrayal of a lesbian relationship could be called
'brilliant … authoritative … truthful … compassionate'.
Both author and critic proved to be (b)s.

From this time dates my growing preoccupation with
the links between a writer's life and work. For many
reasons it had not been easy for me – for any of us – to
identify my sexuality, to fit it into a social, moral and
historical context, to find it clearly delineated and
truthfully explored in literature. Many 19th century male
writers had given lesbianism a mythic quality, sometimes
hostile (Strindberg), sometimes admiring (Gautier).

Others had used it as a symbol of a society or an age, making it represent sterility and cultural exhaustion (Swinburne), the exotic langeurs of some ill defined Hellenistic golden age (Loüys), or a terrifying new breed of woman, heartless, rapacious, unmothering and murderous (Balzac).

The fears and fantasies of those authors, and many others, embodied in works which form part of the canon of Western European classics, had not been helpful to me. They represented a substantial part of the 'knowledge' available to me in a world where there was woefully little reliable and unhostile information. They had made me part of their fiction, without knowing or caring who or what I was. In the process they had helped to distort my own sense of myself. Their reputations as Great Writers gave them an authority far greater than any I could claim for myself when I questioned the truthfulness and attacked the dangerous dishonesties of their 'lesbian' creations.

Simply to introduce the words 'truthfulness' and 'dishonesty' immediately plunged me into an age-old debate about the nature of imaginative 'truth' in fiction, but I didn't realise that. My own increasing demand for 'authenticity', a writing based on truths learned through experience rather than empathetic imagination, defined, for those who care about these things, my position in a critical battle which I didn't even know I'd joined. It became increasingly important to me to know the sexuality of those authors creating lesbian characters. Indeed, it became increasingly important to me to know the sexuality of authors. Gradually, drifting through the straggling, ill pruned grapevine, came rumours, revelations, cries of 'Oh, but of *course* she was! Didn't you *know*?' And even, sometimes, 'Oh, but of *course*. She *is!*' There were, apparently, enormous numbers of highly regarded, living – or only just dead – novelists, short story writers and poets who were homosexual. Their identities were open secrets. *Every* body knew. And, the implication was, what everybody knew, anyone could tell. It wasn't so, of course. Years later, as Literary Editor of *Gay News*, I would become wearisomely familiar with all the arguments which claimed that what Everybody knew, nobody must reveal. After all, when one said *Every*body one meant Everybody Who Was All Right, worthy and worldly enough, sensitive and sophisticated enough, cultured and cautious enough to know. Their number included publishers, critics, journalists and fellow authors but never, somehow, anyone as lowly as the Ordinary Reader. That some readers might have everything to gain from the knowledge – that some writers might write better for knowing they knew – was rarely considered and usually contested by those agents and publishers who safeguarded their authors' presumably shameful secret.

And now, 26 years since I stood at the corner of the Strand and Northumberland Avenue, hopelessly insisting that I wanted *that* one, I have a bewildering choice of fictional lesbians, some of them, admittedly, to be found only on the shelves of specialist gay and feminist bookshops, but others pretty comfortably ensconced in W H Smith's and supermarket check-outs. The presses of the English speaking world vie, it seems, to offer me the lesbian of my choice, clothed in whatever genre best suits my mood – science fiction, family saga, historical novel, murder mystery, Mills and Boon, *Bildungsroman*, school story, a little gentle porn.

I find my feelings mixed. I'm glad they're there, of course and play my own part in making sure they are. Not all of it's Great Literature, but I can overlook occasional naiveties or clumsiness in plot and syntax for the pleasures of an immediately recognisable situation and voice. And much of it is fine by anyone's standards. And all of it, by its very existence, demonstrates how far we have come in just 20 years.

Although I didn't know it at the time, my rage and perplexity as an adolescent reader were shared by thousands of other homosexual women and men who loved books too well to let them go on lying. The

Movement which we made later was primarily concerned with truth. 'Coming out' was both a tactical and moral imperative. And we made writing 'come out' as well as people. We helped to bring about that social change which made it possible for biographers of gay subjects to do their job more honestly; made it possible for those critics who cared to display the connections between writers' hitherto concealed sexuality and their work; made it possible for some gay authors to shift their emphasis and begin to write directly to that section of their audience best able to understand some of their most valuable insights. Our growing visibility within the reading population at large persuaded mainstream publishers that it was worth identifying and meeting our needs, persuaded some of our own number that specifically gay and lesbian presses could survive.

Yes, of course, I'm glad it's all there. Yet, paradoxically and ungratefully, I'm also rather glad it wasn't there for the younger me. The urgency of my need to find myself in and through literature carried me to many places which I might never have visited had I been better provided for as a young lesbian reader. That would have been my loss. That so many of the books I came to value most were the product of gay male love is, at one level, an indication of my difficulties: it was so much easier to find gay men in literature, there were more of them and they were less camouflaged. Nowadays, if I were beginning again as an adolescent reader, I could build a sizable lesbian library and never need to read a single book by a gay man. I'm glad I didn't have that option, grateful that I was instead compelled to explore the teasing bonds and barriers which separate and unite homosexual women and men.

Osbert Sitwell notoriously said that he educated himself at home in his holidays from Eton. Like his, many of my most vital lessons have been self-taught. The things I have really needed to know as a lesbian have never been included on the syllabus. Yet in my own sweet way, I somehow seem to have managed to take in a great deal of the literary and cultural knowledge which Britain has traditionally demanded of its elite. A privileged education, some would call it. It was, I would reply, a privilege grounded in deprivation. But then, what's one more paradox amongst so many?

Notes on Contributors

Jon Cook is a lecturer in English Studies at the University of East Anglia. A contributor to *The Left and the Erotic*, (Lawrence & Wishart, 1983) he has also published on romanticism, contemporary poetry and critical and cultural theory.

Richard Dyer teaches Film Studies at the University of Warwick and is currently completing a book on films made by, for and about lesbians and gay men.

Alison Hennegan was born in 1948, graduated from Girton College Cambridge (where she read English) in 1970, was Literary Editor of *Gay News* from 1977-83, and has been Editor of The Women's Press Bookclub since 1984.

Sarah Lefanu is author of *In the Chinks of the World Machine: Feminism and Science Fiction* (The Women's Press, 1988). She is also editor of the science fiction list for The Women's Press.

Sally Munt is currently working on a PhD on genre and feminist fiction at the University of Sussex. She teaches film and lesbian literature in Brighton.

Susannah Radstone is currently teaching film part-time at Ealing College of Higher Education, researching a PhD on women's culture, the women's novel and the women's film, and working on ideas for a book on the perverse imagination.

Amal Treacher is researching a PhD about need and subjectivity through which she is trying to understanding the growing focus and increasing importance put on the interior self.

Elizabeth Wilson started life as an aesthete and is rapidly reverting to that position. In the period between, she joined women's liberation and the communist party and still hopes for red-blooded socialism rather than the designer beige variety. She has written seven books of which *Adorned in Dreams: Fashion and Modernity* (Virago 1985) and *Prisons of Glass*, a novel, (Methuen 1986) are the most recent.